CRYPTO AND BLOCKCHAIN FROM BEGINNER TO MASTERCLASS

Crypto and Blockchain From Beginner to Masterclass

Daniel Wijaya

Daniel Wijaya

DEDICATION

This book is dedicated to all the pioneers, enthusiasts, and curious minds who dare to venture into the fascinating world of cryptocurrency and blockchain technology. To the beginners taking their first steps and the masters refining their craft, may this book serve as a guide and a source of inspiration.

Special thanks to my family and friends for their unwavering support and encouragement throughout this journey. To the readers, thank you for trusting me to be a part of your learning experience.

CONTENTS

Title Page
Dedication
Chapter 1: Introduction — 1
Chapter 2: Background Issues — 6
Chapter 3: Basics of Cryptocurrency — 11
Chapter 4: Basic of Blockchain — 16
Chapter 5: Technology Behind Blockchain — 23
Chapter 6 : Investing in Cryptocurrency — 29
Chapter 7: Security in the World of Cryptocurrency — 36
Chapter 8: Regulation and Policy — 43
Chapter 9: Practical Uses of Blockchain — 50
Chapter 10: Future of Cryptocurrency and Blockchain — 57
Chapter 11: Masterclass : Advanced Strategies for Trading and Investing in Cryptocurrencies — 63
Chapter 12: Tools and Applications for Blockchain Users — 69
Chapter 13: New Sources and Information — 75
Chapter 14: CEX and DEX Applications — 81
Chapter 15: Types of Cryptocurrency Wallets — 88
Chapter 16: Mining and Halving in Cryptocurrency — 93
Chapter 17: The Importance of Narratives in Crypto Investments — 101

Chapter 18: Conclusion	106
Appendix	111
About The Author	117

CHAPTER 1: INTRODUCTION

Introduction to Cryptocurrency and Blockchain

In recent years, the terms "cryptocurrency" and "blockchain" have become increasingly prevalent in discussions about finance, technology, and the future of digital transactions. But what exactly are these concepts, and why are they so significant?

Cryptocurrency, in its simplest form, is digital or virtual currency that uses cryptography for security. Unlike traditional currencies issued by governments (fiat money), cryptocurrencies operate on technology called blockchain, which ensures transparency, security, and decentralization.

Blockchain is a distributed ledger technology that records all transactions across a network of computers. This decentralized approach eliminates the need for intermediaries like banks, making transactions faster, cheaper, and more secure.

In this book, we will explore the fascinating world of cryptocurrencies and blockchain technology, providing a comprehensive guide from basic concepts to advanced applications. Whether you are a beginner or an expert, this guide is designed to equip you with the knowledge and tools to navigate and succeed in the evolving landscape of digital finance.

A Brief History of Cryptocurrency

The story of cryptocurrency begins with the advent of Bitcoin in 2009. Created by an anonymous person or group of people using the pseudonym Satoshi Nakamoto, Bitcoin was introduced as a peer-to-peer electronic cash system that allowed online payments to be sent directly from one party to another without going through a financial institution.

The underlying technology of Bitcoin, the blockchain, ensured that all transactions were transparent, secure, and immutable. This innovation sparked interest and led to the creation of numerous other cryptocurrencies, commonly referred to as altcoins (alternative coins), each with its unique features and use cases.

Why Cryptocurrency and Blockchain Matter

The significance of cryptocurrency and blockchain technology lies in their potential to revolutionize various industries and aspects of daily life:

- **Financial Inclusion**: Cryptocurrencies provide financial services to individuals who do not have access to traditional banking systems.
- **Security and Privacy**: Blockchain technology ensures secure and private transactions, reducing the risk of fraud and hacking.
- **Decentralization**: Removing intermediaries from transactions can reduce costs and increase efficiency.
- **Transparency**: The immutable nature of blockchain records promotes transparency and accountability in various sectors, including finance, supply chain management, and governance.

As we delve deeper into this book, you will gain a comprehensive understanding of how cryptocurrencies and blockchain technology work, their advantages and disadvantages, and how they are shaping the future of the digital world.

Structure of This Book

This book is structured to guide you through the fundamental concepts of cryptocurrency and blockchain technology, gradually advancing to more complex topics. Here's what you can expect in the upcoming chapters:

1. **Basics of Cryptocurrency**: We will explore what cryptocurrencies are, how they work, and the different types of cryptocurrencies available.

2. **Understanding Blockchain Technology**: This chapter will delve into the mechanics of blockchain, its components, and its security features.
3. **Investing in Cryptocurrency**: Learn the essentials of investing in cryptocurrencies, including strategies, risk management, and market analysis.
4. **Security in the Crypto World**: Discover how to secure your digital assets and protect yourself from common threats.
5. **Regulation and Policy**: An overview of the regulatory landscape surrounding cryptocurrencies and blockchain technology.
6. **Real-World Applications of Blockchain**: Explore how blockchain is being used in various industries, from finance to healthcare.
7. **Future of Cryptocurrency and Blockchain**: Insights into the potential future developments and challenges in the crypto and blockchain space.
8. **Advanced Strategies**: For those looking to deepen their knowledge, this chapter covers advanced trading strategies, technical analysis, and emerging technologies.
9. **Tools and Applications for Blockchain Users**: A comprehensive look at the tools, applications, and resources available to blockchain users.
10. **Crypto Wallets**: Understanding the different types of crypto wallets, their advantages, and disadvantages.
11. **Mining and Halving**: A deep dive into the concepts of mining and halving, their importance, and their impact on the market.
12. **Narratives in Crypto Investments**: The importance of understanding market narratives and aligning investments with trending narratives.

As we embark on this journey, remember that the world of cryptocurrency and blockchain is ever-evolving. Staying informed and continuously learning is key to navigating this dynamic landscape successfully.

Financial Inclusion

One of the most transformative aspects of cryptocurrency is its potential to promote financial inclusion. In many parts of the world, especially in developing countries, a significant portion of the population remains unbanked or underbanked, lacking access to basic financial services. Cryptocurrencies can bridge this gap by providing a decentralized financial infrastructure that is accessible to anyone with an internet connection.

Security and Privacy

Traditional financial systems often struggle with issues related to security and privacy. Cyberattacks, data breaches, and identity theft are common concerns. Cryptocurrencies, through the use of cryptographic techniques, offer enhanced security and privacy features. Transactions are secured by complex algorithms, and users have more control over their personal information.

Decentralization

At the heart of cryptocurrency and blockchain technology is the principle of decentralization. Unlike traditional centralized systems, where a single entity has control, decentralized systems distribute control across a network of participants. This not only reduces the risk of single points of failure but also empowers individuals by giving them direct control over their assets and data.

Transparency

Transparency is another key benefit of blockchain technology. All transactions recorded on a blockchain are visible to all participants, providing an unprecedented level of transparency and accountability. This transparency can help reduce fraud, corruption, and other unethical practices in various industries.

Conclusion

In this introductory chapter, we've touched on the basics of cryptocurrency and blockchain, their historical context, and why they are significant. The subsequent chapters will build on this foundation, providing you with a thorough understanding and practical knowledge to engage with this revolutionary technology.

Let's dive in and explore the transformative world of crypto and blockchain!

CHAPTER 2: BACKGROUND ISSUES

What is Fiat Money?

Fiat money is a type of currency that is issued by a government and holds value primarily because the government maintains it and people have faith in its value. Unlike commodity money, which is backed by a physical good such as gold or silver, fiat money has no intrinsic value. Its value is derived from the relationship between supply and demand and the stability of the issuing government.

History of Fiat Money

The concept of fiat money dates back to ancient China, where paper money was used as a medium of exchange. However, modern fiat money began to take shape in the 20th century:

1. **Early Beginnings**: In ancient China during the Tang Dynasty (618–907 AD), the government issued paper money backed by gold reserves.
2. **The Gold Standard**: For many years, most countries adhered to the gold standard, where the value of their currency was directly linked to a specific amount of gold.
3. **Abandonment of the Gold Standard**: In 1971, the United States, under President Richard Nixon, abandoned the gold standard, leading to the adoption of fiat money on a global scale. This shift allowed governments to print money at will, without the need to back it with physical reserves.

Advantages and Disadvantages of Fiat Money

Advantages:

- **Flexibility**: Governments can control the supply of fiat money, which helps in managing economic variables such as inflation and unemployment.
- **Convenience**: It is more convenient to use and carry compared to commodity money.
- **Stability**: When managed properly, fiat money can provide a stable economic environment.

Disadvantages:

- **Inflation Risk**: Overprinting of fiat money can lead to inflation, reducing the currency's purchasing power.
- **Dependency on Government**: The value of fiat money depends on the stability and policies of the issuing government.
- **Lack of Intrinsic Value**: Fiat money has no intrinsic value and is vulnerable to becoming worthless if people lose confidence in the currency.

Problems Arising with Fiat Money

1. **Inflation**
   - **Definition**: Inflation is the rate at which the general level of prices for goods and services rises, leading to a decrease in purchasing power.
   - **Causes**: Inflation can occur when there is an excess supply of money, increased demand for goods and services, or higher production costs.
   - **Impact**: High inflation erodes the value of savings, increases the cost of living, and can lead to economic instability.

2. **Government Control and Centralization**

- **Monetary Policy**: Central banks control the money supply and interest rates, which can lead to manipulation of the economy.
- **Centralization Risks**: Centralized control can result in inefficiencies, corruption, and lack of transparency.

3. **Security and Counterfeiting**
   - **Counterfeiting**: The production of fake currency undermines the trust and value of fiat money.
   - **Security Measures**: Governments invest heavily in anti-counterfeiting measures, but counterfeiters continually find new ways to create fake money.

4. **International Transaction Fees**
   - **Cost**: Cross-border transactions involving fiat money can be expensive due to exchange rates, banking fees, and other charges.
   - **Time**: Traditional international money transfers can be slow, taking several days to process.

Why Cryptocurrency Was Created

1. **Decentralization and Transparency**
   - **Decentralization**: Cryptocurrencies operate on decentralized networks, removing the need for central authorities and reducing the risk of corruption and manipulation.
   - **Transparency**: Blockchain technology ensures that all transactions are recorded on a public ledger, enhancing transparency and accountability.

2. **Security and Privacy**

- **Cryptography:** Cryptocurrencies use advanced cryptographic techniques to secure transactions and control the creation of new units.
- **Privacy:** While transactions are transparent, the identities of the parties involved can remain private, offering a level of anonymity.

3. **Efficiency of Global Transactions**
   - **Speed:** Cryptocurrency transactions can be processed much faster than traditional banking transfers, often within minutes.
   - **Cost:** Transaction fees for cryptocurrencies are generally lower than those for traditional fiat transfers, especially for international payments.

4. **Alternative to Traditional Financial Systems**
   - **Financial Inclusion:** Cryptocurrencies provide financial services to individuals who do not have access to traditional banking systems, particularly in developing countries.
   - **Innovation:** The rise of decentralized finance (DeFi) and smart contracts offers new financial products and services that are more efficient and accessible than traditional systems.

Conclusion

Fiat money, while offering flexibility and convenience, is fraught with issues such as inflation, centralization, counterfeiting, and high transaction costs. Cryptocurrency emerged as a solution to these problems, offering decentralization, enhanced security and privacy, efficient global transactions, and an alternative to traditional financial systems. Understanding these fundamental differences is crucial for appreciating the potential and implications of cryptocurrencies in the modern financial landscape.

CHAPTER 3: BASICS OF CRYPTOCURRENCY

What is Cryptocurrency?

Cryptocurrency is a form of digital or virtual currency that uses cryptography for security. Unlike traditional currencies issued by governments (fiat money), cryptocurrencies operate independently of a central authority. This decentralized nature is one of the key features that differentiate cryptocurrencies from traditional financial systems.

Cryptocurrencies leverage blockchain technology to gain transparency, immutability, and security. Each transaction is recorded on a public ledger called a blockchain, which is maintained by a network of computers (nodes) spread across the globe. This ensures that transactions are secure, transparent, and cannot be altered once they are recorded.

How Cryptocurrency Works

At the core of every cryptocurrency is the blockchain. Here's a simplified explanation of how cryptocurrencies work:

1. **Decentralized Network**: Cryptocurrencies operate on a decentralized network of computers (nodes) that verify and record transactions. This eliminates the need for a central authority like a bank.

2. **Blockchain**: Transactions are grouped into blocks and added to a chain of previous transactions, creating a blockchain. Each block contains a list of transactions and a reference to the previous block, ensuring the integrity and chronological order of the blockchain.

3. **Cryptography**: Advanced cryptographic techniques secure transactions and control the creation of new units of the currency. Public and private keys are used to facilitate transactions, with the public key serving as an address and the private key acting as a password.
4. **Consensus Mechanisms**: To add new blocks to the blockchain, network participants must agree on the validity of transactions. This is achieved through consensus mechanisms like Proof of Work (PoW) and Proof of Stake (PoS).

Types of Cryptocurrencies

There are thousands of cryptocurrencies available today, each with unique features and use cases. Here are the main categories:

1. **Bitcoin (BTC)**
   - **History**: Created by Satoshi Nakamoto in 2009, Bitcoin is the first and most well-known cryptocurrency.
   - **Purpose**: Designed as a peer-to-peer electronic cash system, Bitcoin allows users to send and receive value without intermediaries.
   - **Pros and Cons**:
     - **Pros**: High security, widespread adoption, and strong liquidity.
     - **Cons**: Slow transaction speeds and high energy consumption due to the PoW consensus mechanism.
2. **Altcoins**
   - **Definition**: Any cryptocurrency other than Bitcoin is considered an altcoin (alternative coin). Altcoins aim to improve upon Bitcoin's limitations or provide additional functionalities.

- **Examples:**
  - **Ethereum (ETH):** Known for its smart contract functionality and decentralized applications (dApps).
  - **Litecoin (LTC):** Offers faster transaction times and a different hashing algorithm.
  - **Ripple (XRP):** Focuses on facilitating fast and low-cost international payments.
- **Pros and Cons:**
  - **Pros:** Diverse use cases, innovative features, and potential for high returns.
  - **Cons:** Higher risk and volatility compared to Bitcoin.

3. **Stablecoins**
   - **Definition:** Stablecoins are cryptocurrencies designed to maintain a stable value by pegging them to a reserve of assets, such as fiat currency or commodities.
   - **Types:**
     - **Fiat-collateralized:** Backed by a reserve of fiat currency (e.g., USDT, USDC).
     - **Crypto-collateralized:** Backed by other cryptocurrencies (e.g., DAI).
     - **Non-collateralized:** Use algorithms to maintain stability (e.g., Ampleforth).
   - **Pros and Cons:**
     - **Pros:** Reduced volatility, making

them suitable for transactions and as a store of value.
- **Cons**: Dependence on underlying assets and regulatory scrutiny.

How to Buy and Store Cryptocurrency

1. **Buying Cryptocurrency**
   - **Exchanges**: The most common way to buy cryptocurrency is through exchanges like Binance, Coinbase, and Kraken. These platforms allow users to trade fiat money for cryptocurrencies or exchange one cryptocurrency for another.
   - **Peer-to-Peer (P2P) Transactions**: Some platforms facilitate direct transactions between buyers and sellers without intermediaries.
   - **ATMs**: Cryptocurrency ATMs allow users to buy cryptocurrencies using cash or credit/debit cards.

2. **Storing Cryptocurrency**
   - **Hardware Wallets**: Physical devices that store private keys offline, providing high security. Examples include Ledger and Trezor.
   - **Software Wallets**: Applications or programs that store private keys on a computer or mobile device. Examples include Exodus and Electrum.
   - **Mobile Wallets**: Smartphone applications that offer convenience and portability. Examples include Trust Wallet and Mycelium.
   - **Web Wallets**: Online wallets accessible

through a web browser. Examples include MetaMask and Coinbase Wallet.

- **Paper Wallets**: Physical documents containing private keys and public addresses. They offer high security if stored properly but can be easily lost or damaged.

Conclusion

In this chapter, we have explored the basics of cryptocurrency, including what it is, how it works, the different types of cryptocurrencies, and how to buy and store them. This foundational knowledge will serve as a stepping stone as we delve deeper into the world of cryptocurrency and blockchain in the upcoming chapters.

CHAPTER 4: BASIC OF BLOCKCHAIN

What is Blockchain?

Blockchain is a revolutionary technology that serves as the underlying foundation for cryptocurrencies and various other applications. It is a decentralized digital ledger that records transactions across a network of computers. Each transaction is grouped into a block, and these blocks are linked together in chronological order to form a continuous chain, hence the term "blockchain." This structure ensures that once a transaction is recorded, it cannot be altered without altering all subsequent blocks, providing a high level of security and transparency.

How Blockchain Works

1. **Decentralized Network**
   - Blockchain operates on a decentralized network of nodes (computers) that maintain a copy of the entire ledger. Each node independently verifies and records transactions, ensuring data integrity and security without a central authority.

2. **Blocks and Transactions**
   - Transactions are grouped into blocks, which are then added to the blockchain in a linear, chronological order. Each block contains a list of transactions, a timestamp, and a reference (hash) to the previous block.

3. **Consensus Mechanisms**

- To add a new block to the blockchain, nodes must reach a consensus on the validity of transactions. Common consensus mechanisms include Proof of Work (PoW) and Proof of Stake (PoS).
  - **Proof of Work (PoW):** Nodes (miners) solve complex mathematical problems to validate transactions and add new blocks. This process requires significant computational power and energy.
  - **Proof of Stake (PoS):** Validators are chosen based on the number of coins they hold and are willing to "stake" as collateral. PoS is more energy-efficient compared to PoW.

Key Features of Blockchain

1. **Decentralization**
   - Unlike traditional centralized systems, blockchain is maintained by a distributed network of nodes. This decentralization reduces the risk of single points of failure and enhances security and resilience.

2. **Immutability**
   - Once data is recorded on the blockchain, it is extremely difficult to alter. This immutability ensures the integrity and reliability of the data, making it suitable for applications that require a high level of trust.

3. **Transparency**
   - All transactions on a blockchain are visible to all participants in the network.

This transparency promotes accountability and reduces the likelihood of fraud and corruption.

4. **Security**
   - Blockchain uses advanced cryptographic techniques to secure transactions and protect against tampering. The decentralized nature also makes it resistant to hacking and other cyber threats.

Main Components of Blockchain

1. **Nodes**
   - Nodes are individual computers that participate in the blockchain network, each maintaining a copy of the ledger. Nodes validate and propagate transactions, ensuring the network's security and integrity.

2. **Transactions**
   - Transactions are the transfer of assets or information recorded on the blockchain. Each transaction is verified by nodes and added to a block.

3. **Blocks**
   - Blocks are containers that hold a batch of transactions. Each block includes a reference (hash) to the previous block, creating a chain of blocks.

4. **Consensus Protocols**
   - Consensus protocols are methods used to achieve agreement on the validity of transactions and the state of the blockchain. Common protocols include PoW, PoS, and Delegated Proof of Stake (DPoS).

Types of Blockchains

1. Public Blockchains
- **Overview**: Public blockchains are open to anyone who wants to participate. They are fully decentralized and secure.
- **Examples**: Bitcoin, Ethereum.
- **Pros**: High security, transparency, and resistance to censorship.
- **Cons**: Scalability issues and high energy consumption (especially with PoW).

2. Private Blockchains
- **Overview**: Private blockchains are restricted to a specific group of participants. They are often used by businesses for internal processes.
- **Examples**: Hyperledger Fabric, R3 Corda.
- **Pros**: More control over participants and transactions, improved scalability.
- **Cons**: Less decentralized, potential for reduced security and transparency.

3. Consortium Blockchains
- **Overview**: Consortium blockchains are managed by a group of organizations. They offer a balance between decentralization and control.
- **Examples**: Quorum, Energy Web Foundation.
- **Pros**: Improved scalability, shared control, and collaboration among trusted entities.
- **Cons**: More centralized than public blockchains, requires trust among participants.

Blockchain Security

1. **Cryptographic Hashing**
   - Each block contains a unique hash, a digital fingerprint created using cryptographic algorithms. Any change to the block's data alters the hash, making tampering detectable.

2. **Digital Signatures**
   - Transactions are signed using private keys, ensuring that only the owner of the key can authorize transactions. This prevents unauthorized access and forgery.

3. **Consensus Mechanisms**
   - Consensus mechanisms like PoW and PoS ensure that all participants agree on the state of the blockchain, preventing double-spending and fraud.

4. **Decentralization**
   - The decentralized nature of blockchain reduces the risk of attacks, as there is no single point of failure. Even if some nodes are compromised, the network remains secure.

Real-World Applications of Blockchain

1. **Finance and Banking**
   - **Cross-Border Payments**: Blockchain can facilitate faster, cheaper, and more transparent international transactions by eliminating intermediaries.
   - **Smart Contracts**: Automated contracts that execute when predefined conditions are met, reducing the need for intermediaries and lowering transaction costs.

2. **Supply Chain Management**
   - **Transparency and Traceability**: Blockchain provides an immutable record of transactions, enhancing transparency and traceability in supply chains. This can help combat counterfeiting and improve efficiency.

3. **Healthcare**
   - **Patient Data Management**: Blockchain can securely store and share patient records, ensuring data integrity and privacy while improving accessibility for healthcare providers.

4. **Government and Public Services**
   - **Voting Systems**: Blockchain can provide a transparent, secure, and immutable voting system, ensuring the integrity of elections.
   - **Land Registration**: Blockchain can provide a tamper-proof system for recording land ownership and transactions, reducing fraud and corruption.

5. **Energy Sector**
   - **Energy Trading**: Blockchain can enable peer-to-peer energy trading, allowing consumers to buy and sell energy directly, improving efficiency and reducing costs.
   - **Renewable Energy Certificates**: Blockchain can provide a transparent and secure way to issue and track renewable energy certificates, ensuring their authenticity.

6. **Intellectual Property**
   - **Rights Management**: Blockchain can provide a transparent and immutable

record of ownership and usage rights, simplifying rights management and royalty distribution.

- **Content Monetization**: Blockchain can facilitate direct transactions between creators and consumers, ensuring fair compensation and reducing intermediaries.

Conclusion

In this chapter, we have explored the basics of blockchain technology, including how it works, its key features, main components, types, security measures, and real-world applications. Understanding these fundamentals provides a solid foundation for delving deeper into the potential and implications of blockchain technology in various industries. In the next chapter, we will discuss investment strategies in cryptocurrency, including essential techniques, risk management, and market analysis.

CHAPTER 5: TECHNOLOGY BEHIND BLOCKCHAIN

Distributed Consensus

Distributed consensus is a fundamental principle in blockchain technology that ensures all participants in a decentralized network agree on the state of the blockchain. This consensus is critical for maintaining the integrity, security, and reliability of the blockchain without the need for a central authority.

1. **Definition**
   - Distributed consensus is a process used to achieve agreement among distributed nodes on the state of the blockchain. It ensures that all nodes have a consistent view of the blockchain, despite potential faults or malicious activities.

2. **Importance**
   - Ensures data integrity and consistency across the network.
   - Prevents double-spending and fraud.
   - Facilitates trustless transactions by eliminating the need for intermediaries.

3. **Mechanisms**
   - Various consensus mechanisms are used to achieve distributed consensus, with the most common being Proof of Work (PoW) and Proof of Stake (PoS).

Proof of Work (PoW) vs. Proof of Stake (PoS)

Proof of Work (PoW) and Proof of Stake (PoS) are two of the most widely used consensus mechanisms in blockchain technology. Each has its own method of achieving consensus and securing the network.

1. **Proof of Work (PoW)**
   - **Overview**: PoW requires miners to solve complex mathematical puzzles to validate transactions and add new blocks to the blockchain.
   - **Process**:
     - Miners compete to solve a cryptographic puzzle.
     - The first miner to solve the puzzle adds the new block to the blockchain and receives a reward (block reward).
   - **Advantages**:
     - High security: The computational power required makes it difficult to attack the network.
     - Proven track record: Used by Bitcoin and other major cryptocurrencies.
   - **Disadvantages**:
     - Energy-intensive: Requires significant electricity consumption.
     - Slower transaction times and scalability issues.

2. **Proof of Stake (PoS)**
   - **Overview**: PoS selects validators based on the number of coins they hold and are willing to "stake" as collateral.

- **Process**:
    - Validators are chosen to create new blocks and validate transactions based on their stake.
    - The likelihood of being chosen increases with the amount of staked coins.
- **Advantages**:
    - Energy-efficient: Does not require extensive computational power.
    - Faster transaction times and better scalability.
- **Disadvantages**:
    - Potential centralization: Wealthier participants with more coins have greater influence.
    - Less proven security: Newer compared to PoW, with fewer large-scale implementations.

Smart Contracts

Smart contracts are self-executing contracts with the terms of the agreement directly written into code. They automatically execute and enforce the terms when predefined conditions are met, eliminating the need for intermediaries.

1. **Definition**
    - Smart contracts are programmable contracts that automatically execute, control, or document legally relevant events and actions according to the terms of the contract.
2. **How They Work**
    - Written in code and deployed on a

blockchain.
- Execute automatically when specified conditions are met.
- Ensure trust and transparency, as all participants can view the contract and its execution.

3. **Advantages**
   - **Automation**: Reduces the need for intermediaries, lowering costs and increasing efficiency.
   - **Transparency**: Terms and execution are transparent and immutable.
   - **Security**: Encrypted and stored on the blockchain, making them tamper-proof.

4. **Use Cases**
   - **Financial Services**: Automated payments, insurance claims, and lending.
   - **Supply Chain**: Tracking and verifying the provenance of goods.
   - **Legal Agreements**: Automating legal processes such as contract enforcement and property transfers.

Decentralized Applications (dApps)

Decentralized applications (dApps) are applications that run on a blockchain network rather than a centralized server. They leverage the features of blockchain to provide transparency, security, and trust.

1. **Definition**
   - dApps are open-source applications that run on a decentralized blockchain network. They use smart contracts to execute their operations and interact with the blockchain.

2. **Characteristics**
    - **Open Source**: The source code is publicly available and can be audited.
    - **Decentralized**: Operate on a blockchain, eliminating single points of failure.
    - **Incentivized**: Users and developers are often incentivized with tokens.

3. **Advantages**
    - **Censorship-Resistant**: Cannot be easily shut down or controlled by a single entity.
    - **Trustless**: Operate without the need for trusted intermediaries.
    - **Transparent**: All transactions and operations are recorded on the blockchain, ensuring transparency.

4. **Challenges**
    - **Scalability**: Current blockchain networks may struggle with large-scale dApp usage.
    - **User Experience**: dApps can be less user-friendly compared to traditional applications.
    - **Regulatory Uncertainty**: The regulatory environment for dApps is still evolving.

5. **Examples**
    - **DeFi Platforms**: Decentralized finance applications like Uniswap, Aave, and Compound.
    - **Gaming**: Blockchain-based games like CryptoKitties and Axie Infinity.
    - **Social Networks**: Decentralized social media platforms like Steemit.

Conclusion

In this chapter, we explored the technology behind blockchain, including distributed consensus mechanisms, the differences between Proof of Work and Proof of Stake, the concept and benefits of smart contracts, and the rise of decentralized applications (dApps). Understanding these technologies is essential for grasping the full potential of blockchain and its applications in various industries. In the next chapter, we will discuss the real-world applications of blockchain technology and how it is transforming different sectors.

CHAPTER 6 : INVESTING IN CRYPTOCURRENCY

Guide to Starting Cryptocurrency Investments

Investing in cryptocurrency can be an exciting but daunting venture. Here's a step-by-step guide to help you get started:

1. **Research and Education**
   - Learn about different cryptocurrencies, blockchain technology, and the market dynamics.
   - Use resources like books, online courses, and reputable websites to build your knowledge.
2. **Choose a Reliable Exchange**
   - Select a reputable cryptocurrency exchange where you can buy and sell cryptocurrencies.
   - Popular exchanges include Coinbase, Binance, and Kraken.
3. **Set Up a Wallet**
   - Use a secure wallet to store your cryptocurrencies. Options include hardware wallets, software wallets, and mobile wallets.
   - Examples: Ledger (hardware), Exodus (software), Trust Wallet (mobile).
4. **Secure Your Investments**
   - Enable two-factor authentication (2FA) on

your accounts.
- Keep your private keys secure and never share them with anyone.

5. **Start Small**
   - Begin with a small investment to understand the market and gain experience.
   - Gradually increase your investment as you become more comfortable.

Understanding the Market

1. **Market Capitalization**
   - The total value of all coins in circulation for a particular cryptocurrency.
   - Indicates the size and popularity of the cryptocurrency.

2. **Volume**
   - The amount of a cryptocurrency that has been traded over a specific period, typically 24 hours.
   - High volume often indicates high liquidity and investor interest.

3. **Volatility**
   - The extent to which the price of a cryptocurrency fluctuates.
   - Cryptocurrencies are known for their high volatility, which can lead to significant price swings.

Key Investment Strategies

1. **HODLing**
   - Buying and holding onto a cryptocurrency for an extended period, regardless of market fluctuations.

- Based on the belief that the long-term value of the cryptocurrency will increase.

2. **Day Trading**
   - Buying and selling cryptocurrencies within a single day to take advantage of short-term price movements.
   - Requires significant time, attention, and technical analysis skills.

3. **Swing Trading**
   - Holding onto a cryptocurrency for several days or weeks to capitalize on expected upward or downward market movements.
   - Uses both technical and fundamental analysis to make informed decisions.

4. **Diversification**
   - Spreading investments across multiple cryptocurrencies to reduce risk.
   - Helps mitigate losses if one particular asset performs poorly.

Technical Analysis vs. Fundamental Analysis

1. **Technical Analysis**
   - **Definition**: Studying historical price data and chart patterns to predict future price movements.
   - **Tools**: Moving averages, RSI, Bollinger Bands, support and resistance levels.

2. **Fundamental Analysis**
   - **Definition**: Evaluating a cryptocurrency's intrinsic value by examining various factors.
   - **Factors**: Technology, development team, adoption, use case, community support.

Risk Management in Cryptocurrency Investment

1. **Invest Only What You Can Afford to Lose**
   - Given the high volatility of cryptocurrencies, it's essential to invest only disposable income.
2. **Set Stop-Loss Orders**
   - Automatically sell your cryptocurrency when it reaches a predetermined price to limit losses.
3. **Keep Emotions in Check**
   - Remain rational and stick to your investment strategy, avoiding impulsive decisions based on emotions.
4. **Regularly Review Your Portfolio**
   - Periodically assess your investments to ensure they align with your financial goals and market conditions.

Legal and Tax Considerations

1. **Regulations**
   - Cryptocurrency regulations vary by country. Ensure you understand the legal requirements in your jurisdiction.
2. **Taxes**
   - In many countries, cryptocurrency transactions are subject to taxation. Keep detailed records of your transactions and consult with a tax professional.

Market Trends and Predictions

1. **Bull and Bear Markets**
   - **Bull Market**: Period of rising prices and investor optimism.

- **Bear Market**: Period of falling prices and investor pessimism.

2. **Market Cycles**
   - Cryptocurrencies often experience cyclical trends, including periods of rapid growth followed by corrections.

3. **Predictions**
   - Stay informed about market predictions from reputable analysts and experts, but always do your own research and due diligence.

Tools and Resources for Investors

1. **Market Data Platforms**
   - **CoinMarketCap**: Provides real-time data on cryptocurrency prices, market capitalization, and volume.
     - **Website**: CoinMarketCap
   - **CoinGecko**: Comprehensive data aggregator with additional metrics such as developer activity and community growth.
     - **Website**: CoinGecko

2. **News Outlets**
   - **CoinDesk**: Leading news site for cryptocurrency and blockchain news, analysis, and insights.
     - **Website**: CoinDesk
   - **CryptoSlate**: Provides news, analysis, and market data on cryptocurrencies and blockchain projects.
     - **Website**: CryptoSlate

3. **Technical Analysis Tools**
   - **TradingView**: Offers charting tools and

technical indicators to aid in analysis.
- **Website**: TradingView
- **CryptoCompare**: Provides a range of data and analysis tools for cryptocurrencies.
  - **Website**: CryptoCompare

4. **Wallets**
   - **Ledger**: Hardware wallet known for its security and support for multiple cryptocurrencies.
     - **Website**: Ledger
   - **Exodus**: Multi-currency software wallet with an intuitive interface.
     - **Website**: Exodus
   - **Trust Wallet**: Mobile wallet that supports multiple cryptocurrencies and integrates with decentralized applications (dApps).
     - **Website**: Trust Wallet

Importance of Understanding Narratives in Investment

1. **What is a Narrative?**
   - A market narrative is a story or theme that captures the collective belief of investors, developers, and users about the future potential and value of a particular technology or asset.

2. **How Narratives Influence Investments**
   - Narratives shape investor behavior, influence price movements, and drive the adoption of specific technologies.
   - Examples: Bitcoin as "digital gold," Ethereum as the "world computer," DeFi as the future of finance.

3. **Identifying and Following Narrative Trends**

- **Research and Information Sources**: Follow reputable cryptocurrency news sites, social media discussions, and industry reports.
- **Key Indicators**: Developer activity, partnerships, market trends, and community sentiment.
- **Evaluating Narratives**: Assess the technology viability, market potential, and current and potential adoption.

Conclusion

Investing in cryptocurrency requires a solid understanding of the market, effective strategies, and robust risk management practices. By leveraging the right tools and resources, staying informed about legal and tax considerations, and understanding market narratives, investors can make informed decisions and navigate the volatile crypto market with confidence. In the next chapter, we will delve into the tools and applications available for blockchain users.

CHAPTER 7: SECURITY IN THE WORLD OF CRYPTOCURRENCY

Importance of Security in Cryptocurrency

Security is a paramount concern in the world of cryptocurrency. Due to the decentralized and digital nature of cryptocurrencies, they are attractive targets for hackers and fraudsters. Ensuring the security of your digital assets is crucial to protect against potential losses and unauthorized access.

1. **Protecting Your Investment**
   - Cryptocurrencies are stored digitally, making them susceptible to hacking, phishing, and other cyber threats.
   - Unlike traditional financial systems, transactions are irreversible, meaning lost or stolen funds are often unrecoverable.

2. **Maintaining Trust in the Ecosystem**
   - Security breaches can undermine trust in the cryptocurrency ecosystem, leading to reduced adoption and market confidence.
   - Strong security practices help build and maintain trust among users and investors.

Common Security Threats

1. **Phishing Attacks**
   - **Definition:** Phishing involves tricking

individuals into providing sensitive information, such as private keys or login credentials, through deceptive emails or websites.

- **Impact**: Once attackers obtain your information, they can access your accounts and steal your funds.

2. **Malware**

   - **Definition**: Malware is malicious software designed to infiltrate and damage or disrupt computer systems.
   - **Types**: Keyloggers (record keystrokes), ransomware (locks data until a ransom is paid), and spyware (steals sensitive information).

3. **Social Engineering**

   - **Definition**: Social engineering involves manipulating individuals into divulging confidential information through psychological manipulation.
   - **Methods**: Impersonating trusted contacts, creating fake support accounts, or offering fake investment opportunities.

4. **Exchange Hacks**

   - **Definition**: Centralized cryptocurrency exchanges are prime targets for hackers due to the large volume of assets they hold.
   - **Examples**: High-profile exchanges like Mt. Gox and Bitfinex have been compromised, leading to significant losses.

5. **SIM Swapping**

   - **Definition**: SIM swapping involves transferring your phone number to a new

SIM card controlled by the attacker.
- **Impact**: Attackers can intercept two-factor authentication (2FA) codes sent to your phone, gaining access to your accounts.

Best Practices for Securing Your Cryptocurrency

1. **Use Strong, Unique Passwords**
   - Ensure that you use strong, unique passwords for your exchange accounts, wallets, and email accounts.
   - Consider using a password manager to keep track of your passwords securely.

2. **Enable Two-Factor Authentication (2FA)**
   - Adding an extra layer of security, such as 2FA, makes it more difficult for attackers to gain access to your accounts.
   - Use hardware-based 2FA methods like YubiKey for added security.

3. **Secure Your Private Keys**
   - Private keys should never be shared with anyone. Store them securely using hardware wallets or offline methods.
   - Avoid storing private keys on internet-connected devices.

4. **Be Wary of Phishing Attempts**
   - Always verify the authenticity of websites and emails before entering your credentials.
   - Bookmark important sites and use them directly to avoid phishing links.

5. **Keep Software Updated**
   - Ensure that your operating system, antivirus software, and any cryptocurrency-related software are up-to-date to protect

against vulnerabilities.

6. **Use Hardware Wallets**
    - Hardware wallets are one of the most secure ways to store your cryptocurrency. They keep your private keys offline and are resistant to malware attacks.
    - Examples: Ledger, Trezor.

7. **Regularly Backup Your Wallet**
    - Regular backups of your wallet can protect you against hardware failures and allow you to recover your funds if your device is lost or stolen.
    - Store backups in multiple secure locations.

Types of Crypto Wallets and Their Security

1. **Hardware Wallets**
    - **Examples**: Ledger, Trezor.
    - **Security**: High; private keys are stored offline, immune to malware.
    - **Pros**: Very secure, supports multiple cryptocurrencies, resistant to hacking.
    - **Cons**: Initial cost, requires physical storage and safekeeping.

2. **Software Wallets**
    - **Examples**: Exodus, Electrum.
    - **Security**: Moderate; keys are stored on your computer or mobile device.
    - **Pros**: Easy to use, convenient, supports various cryptocurrencies.
    - **Cons**: Vulnerable to malware and hacking if the device is compromised.

3. **Mobile Wallets**

- **Examples**: Trust Wallet, Mycelium.
- **Security**: Moderate; convenient for everyday transactions but can be vulnerable if the phone is lost or stolen.
- **Pros**: Portable, easy to use, supports various cryptocurrencies.
- **Cons**: Risk of loss or theft of the mobile device.

4. **Web Wallets**
   - **Examples**: MetaMask, Coinbase Wallet.
   - **Security**: Variable; depends on the security measures of the web service.
   - **Pros**: Accessible from any device with internet, easy to use.
   - **Cons**: Vulnerable to phishing attacks, reliant on the security of the web service.

5. **Paper Wallets**
   - **Security**: High if stored properly; private keys are written on paper.
   - **Pros**: Not connected to the internet, immune to online threats.
   - **Cons**: Susceptible to physical damage or loss, requires careful handling.

6. **Multi-Signature Wallets**
   - **Definition**: Wallets that require multiple private keys to authorize a transaction.
   - **Security**: Enhanced; multiple keys reduce the risk of unauthorized access.
   - **Pros**: Shared control, useful for organizations or joint accounts.
   - **Cons**: Complex setup, requires coordination among multiple parties.

Scams and Ponzi Schemes in Cryptocurrency

1. **Ponzi Schemes**
   - **Definition**: Investment scams that promise high returns with little risk. New investor funds are used to pay earlier investors.
   - **Warning Signs**: High, guaranteed returns, lack of transparency, pressure to recruit new investors.

2. **Fake ICOs and Token Sales**
   - **Definition**: Fraudulent initial coin offerings (ICOs) and token sales designed to steal investors' money.
   - **Warning Signs**: Lack of a clear project plan, anonymous team members, unrealistic promises.

3. **Pump and Dump Schemes**
   - **Definition**: Coordinated efforts to artificially inflate the price of a cryptocurrency before selling off holdings at a profit.
   - **Warning Signs**: Sudden, unexplained price increases, coordinated social media promotion.

4. **Phishing and Social Engineering**
   - **Methods**: Fake websites, emails, or messages designed to trick you into revealing private information.
   - **Prevention**: Verify sources, use bookmarks, and avoid clicking on suspicious links.

Dealing with Lost or Stolen Cryptocurrency

1. **Contact the Exchange**
   - If the theft occurred through an exchange, contact their support team immediately for

assistance.

2. **Report the Incident**
   - Report the theft to the relevant authorities. Some jurisdictions have cybercrime units that can assist.

3. **Notify the Community**
   - Inform the cryptocurrency community about the theft. This can sometimes help track the stolen funds.

4. **Improve Security Practices**
   - Learn from the incident and implement stronger security measures to prevent future losses.

Conclusion

In this chapter, we have explored the importance of security in the cryptocurrency world, common security threats, best practices for securing your assets, different types of wallets and their security, common scams and Ponzi schemes, and steps to take if your cryptocurrency is lost or stolen. By implementing strong security measures and staying vigilant, you can protect your investments and navigate the cryptocurrency space with confidence. In the next chapter, we will discuss the tools and applications available for blockchain users.

CHAPTER 8: REGULATION AND POLICY

Overview of Cryptocurrency Regulation

Cryptocurrency regulation is a rapidly evolving field as governments and regulatory bodies worldwide attempt to address the unique challenges and opportunities presented by digital currencies and blockchain technology. Regulations aim to ensure market integrity, protect consumers, and prevent illegal activities such as money laundering and fraud.

Cryptocurrency Regulations in Various Countries

1. **United States**
    - **Securities and Exchange Commission (SEC)**: Oversees securities regulation, including determining whether certain cryptocurrencies and initial coin offerings (ICOs) qualify as securities.
    - **Commodity Futures Trading Commission (CFTC)**: Regulates derivatives markets and has classified Bitcoin and Ethereum as commodities.
    - **Internal Revenue Service (IRS)**: Treats cryptocurrencies as property for tax purposes, meaning capital gains tax applies to transactions.
    - **Financial Crimes Enforcement Network (FinCEN)**: Enforces anti-money laundering (AML) and know your customer (KYC)

regulations.

2. **European Union**
   - **European Securities and Markets Authority (ESMA):** Provides guidance on how existing financial regulations apply to cryptocurrencies.
   - **Fifth Anti-Money Laundering Directive (5AMLD):** Requires cryptocurrency exchanges and wallet providers to comply with AML and KYC regulations.
   - **Markets in Crypto-Assets Regulation (MiCA):** Proposed regulation aimed at providing a comprehensive regulatory framework for crypto assets within the EU.

3. **Japan**
   - **Financial Services Agency (FSA):** Regulates cryptocurrency exchanges and enforces strict AML and KYC requirements. Japan was one of the first countries to recognize Bitcoin as legal tender.
   - **Japan Virtual Currency Exchange Association (JVCEA):** A self-regulatory organization that sets standards and practices for the industry.

4. **China**
   - **People's Bank of China (PBoC):** Has implemented stringent regulations, including banning cryptocurrency exchanges and ICOs. However, China is actively developing its own central bank digital currency (CBDC).
   - **Mining Restrictions:** China has also cracked down on cryptocurrency mining activities

within its borders.

5. **Singapore**
   - **Monetary Authority of Singapore (MAS)**: Provides a favorable regulatory environment, with clear guidelines and support for innovation. The Payment Services Act regulates payment services, including cryptocurrency exchanges and wallets.

6. **Switzerland**
   - **Swiss Financial Market Supervisory Authority (FINMA)**: Implements progressive regulations to attract blockchain and cryptocurrency businesses, particularly in "Crypto Valley" in Zug.
   - **Blockchain Act**: Provides a legal framework for blockchain and distributed ledger technology (DLT) applications.

Key Regulatory Issues

1. **Classification of Cryptocurrencies**
   - Determining whether cryptocurrencies should be classified as securities, commodities, or another asset class affects how they are regulated and taxed.

2. **Anti-Money Laundering (AML) and Know Your Customer (KYC) Compliance**
   - Ensuring that cryptocurrency transactions are not used for money laundering or financing terrorism is a primary concern for regulators.
   - Exchanges and wallet providers are often required to implement robust AML and KYC procedures.

3. **Consumer Protection**
   - Protecting investors from fraud, scams, and market manipulation is a significant regulatory focus.
   - Regulators seek to ensure transparency and fair practices in the market.

4. **Taxation**
   - How cryptocurrencies are taxed varies by jurisdiction, with implications for individuals and businesses.
   - Issues include capital gains tax, income tax on mining rewards, and reporting requirements.

5. **Privacy and Data Protection**
   - Balancing the privacy features of cryptocurrencies with regulatory requirements for transparency and accountability is a challenge.
   - Regulations like the General Data Protection Regulation (GDPR) in the EU impact how personal data is handled in the crypto space.

The Impact of Regulation on The Crypto Market

1. **Positive Impacts**
   - **Increased Legitimacy**: Clear regulatory frameworks can enhance the legitimacy of cryptocurrencies and attract institutional investors.
   - **Consumer Protection**: Regulations can help protect consumers from fraud and ensure fair market practices.
   - **Market Stability**: Regulatory oversight can reduce volatility and promote stability in

the market.

2. **Negative Impacts**
   - **Compliance Costs**: Regulatory compliance can be costly and complex, particularly for startups and smaller businesses.
   - **Innovation Constraints**: Overly stringent regulations may stifle innovation and hinder the development of new technologies and business models.
   - **Market Access**: Inconsistent regulations across different jurisdictions can create barriers to entry and complicate cross-border transactions.

Future Trends in Cryptocurrency Regulation

1. **Global Coordination**
   - As cryptocurrencies are inherently global, there is an increasing need for international regulatory coordination to address cross-border issues and ensure consistent standards.

2. **Central Bank Digital Currencies (CBDCs)**
   - Many central banks are exploring the development of their own digital currencies, which could coexist with or compete against decentralized cryptocurrencies.
   - CBDCs could enhance payment efficiency, reduce costs, and provide central banks with new tools for monetary policy.

3. **Regulatory Sandboxes**
   - Some countries are implementing regulatory sandboxes that allow startups to experiment with new technologies and business models under regulatory

supervision.
- Sandboxes provide a controlled environment to test the impact of new regulations and innovations.

4. **Decentralized Finance (DeFi)**
   - The rise of DeFi platforms presents new regulatory challenges, as they operate without traditional intermediaries and can be difficult to regulate.
   - Regulators are exploring how to apply existing financial regulations to DeFi and address associated risks.

Navigating Regulatory Compliance

1. **Stay Informed**
   - Keep up-to-date with the latest regulatory developments in your jurisdiction and globally.
   - Follow news outlets, industry reports, and regulatory announcements.

2. **Seek Legal Advice**
   - Consult with legal experts who specialize in cryptocurrency and blockchain to ensure compliance with relevant laws and regulations.
   - Consider the regulatory environment when selecting markets and business models.

3. **Implement Best Practices**
   - Adopt best practices for AML, KYC, and consumer protection to minimize regulatory risks.
   - Develop robust compliance programs and internal controls.

4. **Engage with Regulators**
    - Participate in industry groups and engage with regulators to contribute to the development of fair and effective regulations.
    - Provide feedback on proposed regulations and advocate for balanced approaches.

Conclusion

In this chapter, we have explored the complex and evolving regulatory landscape surrounding cryptocurrencies and blockchain technology. Understanding the regulatory environment is crucial for navigating the opportunities and challenges in the crypto space. By staying informed, seeking legal advice, and implementing best practices, individuals and businesses can ensure compliance and contribute to the sustainable growth of the cryptocurrency ecosystem. In the next chapter, we will examine the real-world applications of blockchain technology and how it is transforming various industries.

CHAPTER 9: PRACTICAL USES OF BLOCKCHAIN

Blockchain in the Financial Industry

Blockchain technology has had a profound impact on the financial industry, offering new ways to enhance security, transparency, and efficiency. Here are some key applications:

1. **Cross-Border Payments**
   - **Current Challenges**: Traditional cross-border payments are often slow, expensive, and involve multiple intermediaries.
   - **Blockchain Solution**: Blockchain can facilitate faster, cheaper, and more transparent international transactions by eliminating intermediaries and reducing settlement times.
   - **Examples**: Ripple (XRP) enables real-time cross-border payments with reduced fees. Stellar (XLM) focuses on low-cost, cross-border transactions for the unbanked.

2. **Smart Contracts**
   - **Definition**: Smart contracts are self-executing contracts with the terms of the agreement directly written into code.
   - **Applications**: They can automate and enforce agreements without the need for intermediaries, reducing costs and increasing efficiency.

- **Examples**: Ethereum is the leading platform for smart contracts, enabling decentralized applications (dApps) and automated financial agreements.

3. **Decentralized Finance (DeFi)**
   - **Overview**: DeFi refers to financial services built on blockchain that operate without traditional intermediaries like banks.
   - **Key Services**: These include lending, borrowing, trading, and earning interest on crypto assets.
   - **Examples**: Uniswap (decentralized exchange), Aave (lending platform), and Compound (interest-earning platform).

4. **Tokenization of Assets**
   - **Definition**: Tokenization involves creating digital tokens that represent ownership of real-world assets, such as real estate, stocks, or art.
   - **Benefits**: Increases liquidity, allows fractional ownership, and simplifies the transfer of assets.
   - **Examples**: Platforms like Polymath and Tokeny facilitate the tokenization of traditional assets.

Blockchain in Supply Chain Management

Blockchain technology can significantly enhance supply chain management by improving transparency, traceability, and efficiency.

1. **Transparency and Traceability**
   - **Current Challenges**: Supply chains are often complex, involving multiple parties and a lack of transparency, leading to

inefficiencies and fraud.
- **Blockchain Solution**: Blockchain provides an immutable record of transactions and product journeys, enhancing transparency and traceability.
- **Examples**: IBM Food Trust uses blockchain to trace the origin and journey of food products, ensuring safety and authenticity. VeChain offers supply chain solutions for various industries, including luxury goods and pharmaceuticals.

2. **Counterfeit Prevention**
   - **Problem**: Counterfeit goods are a significant issue in many industries, including pharmaceuticals, luxury goods, and electronics.
   - **Solution**: Blockchain can authenticate the origin and journey of products, making it harder for counterfeit items to enter the supply chain.
   - **Examples**: Everledger uses blockchain to track the provenance of diamonds and other high-value goods, reducing the risk of counterfeiting.

3. **Efficiency Improvements**
   - **Current Challenges**: Traditional supply chain processes are often slow and inefficient, with significant paperwork and manual intervention.
   - **Blockchain Solution**: Smart contracts can automate processes such as payments, order processing, and customs clearance, improving efficiency and reducing costs.

- **Examples**: TradeLens, a blockchain platform developed by Maersk and IBM, aims to streamline global trade by digitizing supply chain processes.

Blockchain in Government

Blockchain technology has the potential to transform various government functions by enhancing transparency, security, and efficiency.

1. **Voting Systems**
   - **Current Challenges**: Traditional voting systems can be vulnerable to fraud, manipulation, and inefficiencies.
   - **Blockchain Solution**: Blockchain can provide a transparent, secure, and immutable voting system, ensuring the integrity of elections.
   - **Examples**: Follow My Vote and Horizon State are developing blockchain-based voting platforms to ensure secure and transparent elections.

2. **Land Registration**
   - **Problem**: Land registries can be prone to fraud, corruption, and inefficiencies.
   - **Solution**: Blockchain can provide a transparent and tamper-proof system for recording land ownership and transactions.
   - **Examples**: The government of Georgia has implemented a blockchain-based land registry system to reduce fraud and increase efficiency.

3. **Identity Management**
   - **Current Challenges**: Traditional identity management systems can be inefficient,

insecure, and prone to fraud.
- **Blockchain Solution**: Blockchain can provide a secure and decentralized way to manage identities, reducing the risk of identity theft and fraud.
- **Examples**: ID2020 and uPort are working on blockchain-based identity solutions to provide secure and verifiable digital identities.

4. **Public Records**
   - **Problem**: Managing public records, such as birth certificates, marriage licenses, and academic credentials, can be inefficient and vulnerable to tampering.
   - **Solution**: Blockchain can provide a secure and immutable system for managing public records.
   - **Examples**: The city of Dubai is implementing a blockchain strategy to digitize and secure all government documents and transactions.

Blockchain in the Healthcare Sector

Blockchain technology can address several critical issues in the healthcare sector, including data security, interoperability, and supply chain management.

1. **Patient Data Management**
   - **Current Challenges**: Managing patient records is often fragmented, leading to inefficiencies and privacy concerns.
   - **Blockchain Solution**: Blockchain can provide a secure, unified, and tamper-proof system for storing and sharing patient records, ensuring data integrity and privacy.

- **Examples**: Medicalchain and Patientory are exploring blockchain applications for secure and interoperable patient data management.

2. **Drug Traceability**
    - **Problem**: Ensuring the authenticity and safety of drugs is a critical issue.
    - **Solution**: Blockchain can track the production, distribution, and delivery of pharmaceuticals, reducing the risk of counterfeit drugs.
    - **Examples**: Chronicled uses blockchain to provide end-to-end traceability of pharmaceuticals, ensuring their authenticity and safety.

3. **Clinical Trials**
    - **Current Challenges**: Clinical trials often suffer from data manipulation, lack of transparency, and inefficiencies.
    - **Blockchain Solution**: Blockchain can provide a transparent and tamper-proof record of clinical trial data, ensuring integrity and compliance.
    - **Examples**: PharmaLedger is a consortium project aimed at using blockchain to enhance the transparency and efficiency of clinical trials.

4. **Medical Billing and Claims**
    - **Problem**: Medical billing and claims processes are often complex, slow, and prone to errors and fraud.
    - **Solution**: Blockchain can automate and streamline medical billing and claims

processes, reducing errors and fraud.
- **Examples**: Solve.Care uses blockchain to improve the efficiency and transparency of healthcare administration and billing processes.

Conclusion

In this chapter, we have explored the practical uses of blockchain technology across various sectors, including finance, supply chain management, government, and healthcare. Blockchain's potential to enhance transparency, security, and efficiency makes it a powerful tool for addressing many of the challenges faced by these industries. By understanding and leveraging these applications, organizations can unlock significant value and drive innovation in their respective fields. In the next chapter, we will discuss future trends in cryptocurrency and blockchain, examining potential developments and the challenges that lie ahead.

CHAPTER 10: FUTURE OF CRYPTOCURRENCY AND BLOCKCHAIN

Emerging Trends in Cryptocurrency

The cryptocurrency landscape is constantly evolving, driven by technological advancements, regulatory developments, and changing market dynamics. Here are some of the key emerging trends:

1. **Central Bank Digital Currencies (CBDCs)**
   - **Overview**: Central banks around the world are exploring the development of their own digital currencies to complement or replace traditional fiat currencies.
   - **Examples**: China's digital yuan, the European Central Bank's digital euro, and discussions around a digital dollar in the United States.
   - **Implications**: CBDCs could enhance payment efficiency, reduce costs, and provide central banks with new tools for monetary policy. However, they also raise concerns about privacy and the centralization of digital currency control.

2. **Decentralized Finance (DeFi)**
   - **Growth**: DeFi platforms are rapidly gaining traction, offering financial services like

lending, borrowing, trading, and earning interest without traditional intermediaries.
- **Innovation**: Projects are continually developing new DeFi applications, including decentralized exchanges (DEXs), synthetic assets, and automated market makers (AMMs).
- **Challenges**: DeFi faces regulatory scrutiny, security vulnerabilities, and scalability issues.

3. **Non-Fungible Tokens (NFTs)**
   - **Definition**: NFTs are unique digital assets verified using blockchain technology. They represent ownership of digital or physical items like art, music, and collectibles.
   - **Market Growth**: The NFT market has seen explosive growth, with high-profile sales and increasing mainstream adoption.
   - **Applications**: Beyond art and collectibles, NFTs are being explored for use in gaming, virtual real estate, and digital identity.

4. **Interoperability Solutions**
   - **Need**: As the number of blockchain networks grows, so does the need for them to communicate and interact seamlessly.
   - **Solutions**: Projects like Polkadot, Cosmos, and Chainlink are developing technologies to enable interoperability between different blockchains.
   - **Impact**: Interoperability can enhance the efficiency and functionality of blockchain ecosystems, enabling broader adoption and more complex applications.

Evolution of Blockchain Technology

1. **Scalability Solutions**
   - **Layer 2 Scaling**: Technologies like the Lightning Network for Bitcoin and rollups for Ethereum are being developed to process transactions off the main chain, increasing throughput and reducing fees.
   - **Sharding**: Splitting the blockchain into smaller, manageable pieces (shards) to process transactions in parallel, improving scalability.

2. **Consensus Mechanisms**
   - **Proof of Stake (PoS)**: Ethereum's transition from Proof of Work (PoW) to PoS aims to increase energy efficiency and scalability while maintaining security.
   - **New Mechanisms**: Innovations like Proof of History (PoH) in Solana and Delegated Proof of Stake (DPoS) in EOS are being explored to enhance performance and security.

3. **Privacy Enhancements**
   - **Zero-Knowledge Proofs**: Technologies like zk-SNARKs and zk-STARKs enable transactions to be verified without revealing sensitive information, enhancing privacy.
   - **Confidential Transactions**: Solutions like Monero and Zcash offer enhanced privacy features, making transaction details confidential.

4. **Decentralized Autonomous Organizations (DAOs)**
   - **Definition**: DAOs are organizations governed by smart contracts, allowing decentralized decision-making and

management.
- **Potential**: DAOs could revolutionize governance structures in both the corporate and nonprofit sectors, enabling more democratic and transparent operations.

Future Potential of Cryptocurrency

1. **Mainstream Adoption**
   - **Vision**: Widespread acceptance of blockchain and cryptocurrencies in daily life, from payments to smart contracts and decentralized applications.
   - **Drivers**: Technological advancements, regulatory clarity, and increased consumer and institutional adoption.

2. **Financial Inclusion**
   - **Goal**: Leveraging blockchain to provide financial services to underserved populations, promoting greater economic participation and reducing inequality.

3. **Innovation Hub**
   - **Future**: Blockchain technology serving as a foundation for continuous innovation in various sectors, from finance and healthcare to supply chain management and beyond.

4. **Global Decentralization**
   - **Potential**: A move towards more decentralized global systems, reducing the control of centralized entities over data, finance, and governance.

Challenges and Opportunities Ahead

1. **Regulatory Uncertainty**
   - **Issue**: The regulatory landscape for

cryptocurrencies and blockchain is still evolving, with significant differences between jurisdictions.
- **Impact**: Regulatory uncertainty can hinder innovation and investment. Clear and consistent regulations are needed to support growth while ensuring consumer protection and market integrity.

2. **Security Concerns**
   - **Risks**: Despite the security features of blockchain, the ecosystem is not immune to hacks, fraud, and vulnerabilities. High-profile breaches have raised concerns about the security of digital assets.
   - **Measures**: Enhanced security protocols, regular audits, and responsible development practices are essential to mitigate these risks.

3. **Environmental Impact**
   - **Issue**: The energy consumption of Proof of Work (PoW) cryptocurrencies like Bitcoin has raised environmental concerns.
   - **Solutions**: Transitioning to more energy-efficient consensus mechanisms (e.g., Proof of Stake) and leveraging renewable energy sources for mining.
   - **Balance**: Finding a balance between the security and decentralization benefits of PoW and the environmental impact is critical for sustainable growth.

4. **Scalability**
   - **Problem**: Many blockchain networks face scalability challenges, limiting their ability

to handle a high volume of transactions.
- **Solutions**: Implementing Layer 2 solutions, sharding, and exploring new consensus mechanisms to enhance scalability and performance.

5. **Market Volatility**
   - **Challenge**: The high volatility of cryptocurrencies can deter mainstream adoption and investment.
   - **Opportunity**: As the market matures and stabilizes, it could attract more institutional and retail investors, driving further growth and innovation.

Conclusion

In this chapter, we have explored the future of cryptocurrency and blockchain, examining emerging trends, the evolution of blockchain technology, the future potential of cryptocurrency, and the challenges and opportunities ahead. The dynamic and rapidly evolving nature of this field presents both exciting opportunities and significant challenges. By staying informed, adaptable, and innovative, individuals and businesses can navigate this landscape and contribute to the transformative potential of blockchain and cryptocurrency.

CHAPTER 11: MASTERCLASS : ADVANCED STRATEGIES FOR TRADING AND INVESTING IN CRYPTOCURRENCIES

Advanced Trading and Investment Strategies

As you become more familiar with the basics of cryptocurrency trading and investing, you may want to explore advanced strategies to enhance your returns and manage risks more effectively. Here are several advanced techniques:

1. **Algorithmic Trading**
    - **Definition**: Using computer algorithms to execute trades based on predefined criteria.
    - **Advantages**: Speed, precision, and the ability to backtest strategies.
    - **Strategies**: Arbitrage, market making, trend following, and mean reversion.
    - **Tools**: Trading bots like 3Commas, CryptoHopper, and custom scripts on platforms like TradingView.

2. **Margin Trading**
    - **Definition**: Borrowing funds to increase the size of a trading position.
    - **Risks**: Higher potential for both gains and

losses; understanding margin requirements and managing risk is essential.
- **Platforms**: Binance, BitMEX, and Kraken offer margin trading options.

3. **Options and Futures Trading**
   - **Options**: Contracts that give the right, but not the obligation, to buy or sell an asset at a specific price before a certain date.
   - **Futures**: Agreements to buy or sell an asset at a predetermined price at a specified time in the future.
   - **Advantages**: Allows for hedging and speculation with leveraged positions.
   - **Platforms**: Deribit, CME Group, and Bakkt.

4. **Yield Farming and Staking**
   - **Yield Farming**: Providing liquidity to DeFi platforms in exchange for interest and rewards.
   - **Staking**: Participating in the Proof of Stake (PoS) consensus mechanism by locking up cryptocurrency to support network operations and earning rewards.
   - **Platforms**: Aave, Compound, Uniswap for yield farming; Ethereum 2.0, Cardano for staking.

5. **Swing Trading**
   - **Definition**: Holding onto a cryptocurrency for several days or weeks to capitalize on expected upward or downward market movements.
   - **Analysis**: Uses both technical and fundamental analysis to make informed decisions.

- **Tools**: Technical indicators, chart patterns, and market sentiment analysis.

In-depth Market Analysis

1. **Technical Analysis**
   - **Chart Patterns**: Head and Shoulders, Double Top/Bottom, Triangles (Ascending, Descending, Symmetrical).
   - **Indicators**: Moving Averages (SMA, EMA), Relative Strength Index (RSI), Bollinger Bands, Fibonacci Retracement, MACD.
   - **Volume Analysis**: Understanding the significance of trading volume to confirm trends and identify potential reversals.

2. **Fundamental Analysis**
   - **Project Evaluation**: Assess the project's whitepaper, development team, technology, and use case.
   - **Market Position**: Analyze competitors, market demand, and strategic partnerships.
   - **Tokenomics**: Understand the total supply, circulating supply, and token utility within the ecosystem.

3. **Sentiment Analysis**
   - **Social Media**: Monitor sentiment on platforms like Twitter, Reddit, and Telegram.
   - **News and Events**: Stay updated with the latest news, regulatory developments, and significant events that could impact the market.
   - **On-Chain Metrics**: Analyze blockchain data such as transaction volumes, active

addresses, and network hash rates.

New Technologies in Blockchain and Cryptocurrency

1. **Layer 2 Solutions**
    - **Purpose**: Enhance the scalability and usability of existing blockchain networks by processing transactions off the main chain while retaining the security of the main blockchain.
    - **Examples**: Lightning Network (Bitcoin), Optimistic Rollups and zk-Rollups (Ethereum).

2. **Interoperability Protocols**
    - **Purpose**: Enable seamless communication and transfer of assets between different blockchain networks.
    - **Examples**: Polkadot, Cosmos, and Chainlink.

3. **Privacy Technologies**
    - **Purpose**: Enhance the privacy and confidentiality of blockchain transactions.
    - **Examples**: zk-SNARKs and zk-STARKs (used by Zcash), MimbleWimble (used by Grin and Beam).

4. **Decentralized Identity**
    - **Purpose**: Provide secure and verifiable digital identities on the blockchain.
    - **Examples**: Microsoft's ION, Sovrin, and Civic.

Use Cases and Real-World Case Studies

1. **Supply Chain Management**
    - **Case Study**: IBM Food Trust
        - **Overview**: Uses blockchain to trace the origin and journey of

food products, ensuring safety and authenticity.
- **Impact**: Enhanced transparency, reduced fraud, and improved efficiency in the supply chain.

2. **Healthcare**
   - **Case Study**: MedRec
     - **Overview**: A blockchain-based system for managing electronic medical records.
     - **Impact**: Improved data interoperability, enhanced patient privacy, and streamlined healthcare processes.

3. **Finance**
   - **Case Study**: Ripple (XRP)
     - **Overview**: Facilitates real-time cross-border payments with reduced fees.
     - **Impact**: Increased efficiency in international transactions, reduced costs, and faster settlement times.

4. **Real Estate**
   - **Case Study**: Propy
     - **Overview**: Uses blockchain to streamline the real estate transaction process.
     - **Impact**: Reduced fraud, faster transactions, and increased transparency in property transfers.

5. **Voting Systems**
   - **Case Study**: Follow My Vote

- **Overview**: A blockchain-based voting platform designed to ensure secure and transparent elections.
- **Impact**: Enhanced voter trust, reduced fraud, and improved election integrity.

Conclusion

In this chapter, we have delved into advanced trading and investment strategies, in-depth market analysis, emerging technologies in blockchain and cryptocurrency, and real-world use cases and case studies. By leveraging these advanced techniques and staying informed about the latest developments, you can enhance your trading and investment strategies, capitalize on new opportunities, and navigate the dynamic cryptocurrency market with confidence.

CHAPTER 12: TOOLS AND APPLICATIONS FOR BLOCKCHAIN USERS

Market Information Platforms and Websites

Access to accurate and timely market information is crucial for successful cryptocurrency trading and investment. Here are some of the most popular and reliable platforms and websites for market information:

1. **CoinMarketCap**
   - **Overview**: One of the most widely used platforms for tracking cryptocurrency prices, market capitalizations, trading volumes, and other key metrics.
   - **Features**: Provides real-time data on a wide range of cryptocurrencies, historical price charts, market rankings, and news updates.
   - **Website**: CoinMarketCap

2. **CoinGecko**
   - **Overview**: A comprehensive cryptocurrency data aggregator that offers information on prices, trading volumes, market capitalizations, and more.
   - **Features**: Includes additional metrics such as developer activity, community growth, and liquidity. It also offers a comprehensive DeFi section.

- **Website**: CoinGecko
3. **CryptoSlate**
    - **Overview**: Provides news, analysis, and market data on cryptocurrencies and blockchain projects.
    - **Features**: Offers insights into ICOs, STOs, and other fundraising events. It also covers industry news and provides detailed profiles for various blockchain projects.
    - **Website**: CryptoSlate
4. **Token Terminal**
    - **Overview**: Focuses on financial metrics and fundamental analysis for crypto assets.
    - **Features**: Provides data on revenue, earnings, and user activity for various blockchain projects, allowing users to perform in-depth financial analysis.
    - **Website**: Token Terminal
5. **Chain Broker**
    - **Overview**: A platform that tracks fundraising events, venture capital investments, and project token sales.
    - **Features**: Offers detailed information on funding rounds and participating investors, helping users stay informed about the latest investment trends in the crypto space.
    - **Website**: Chain Broker

Best Cryptocurrency Wallets

Choosing a secure and reliable wallet is essential for managing your cryptocurrency assets. Here are some of the best options available:

1. **Hardware Wallets**

- **Ledger**
  - **Overview**: A leading hardware wallet known for its robust security features and support for multiple cryptocurrencies.
  - **Features**: Offline storage of private keys, support for over 1,500 cryptocurrencies, and integration with various blockchain apps.
  - **Website**: Ledger
- **Trezor**
  - **Overview**: Another popular hardware wallet offering high security and ease of use.
  - **Features**: Supports multiple cryptocurrencies, offers a user-friendly interface, and provides advanced security features.
  - **Website**: Trezor

2. **Software Wallets**
   - **Exodus**
     - **Overview**: A multi-currency wallet with an intuitive interface, designed for desktop and mobile users.
     - **Features**: Built-in exchange, portfolio tracking, and support for a wide range of cryptocurrencies.
     - **Website**: Exodus
   - **Electrum**
     - **Overview**: A lightweight Bitcoin wallet known for its speed and

security.
- **Features**: Advanced features like hardware wallet support, multi-signature wallets, and integration with cold storage.
- **Website**: Electrum

3. **Mobile Wallets**
   - **Trust Wallet**
     - **Overview**: A mobile wallet that supports multiple cryptocurrencies and integrates with decentralized applications (dApps).
     - **Features**: Easy-to-use interface, staking options, and built-in Web3 browser.
     - **Website**: Trust Wallet
   - **Mycelium**
     - **Overview**: A mobile wallet known for its advanced privacy and security features.
     - **Features**: Hardware wallet support, local trader feature, and cold storage options.
     - **Website**: Mycelium

4. **Web Wallets**
   - **MetaMask**
     - **Overview**: A popular web wallet and browser extension that allows users to interact with Ethereum-based dApps.
     - **Features**: Secure key management, support for ERC-20 tokens, and

integration with various DeFi platforms.
- **Website**: MetaMask
- **Coinbase Wallet**
  - **Overview**: A user-friendly web wallet provided by the Coinbase exchange.
  - **Features**: Supports multiple cryptocurrencies, integrates with dApps, and offers a secure storage solution.
  - **Website**: Coinbase Wallet

Analysis and Portfolio Management Tools

Effective analysis and portfolio management tools are essential for making informed investment decisions and tracking your cryptocurrency assets. Here are some of the best tools available:

1. **TradingView**
   - **Overview**: A comprehensive charting platform that offers a wide range of technical analysis tools.
   - **Features**: Customizable charts, technical indicators, drawing tools, and social features that allow users to share ideas and strategies.
   - **Website**: TradingView
2. **CoinTracking**
   - **Overview**: A portfolio management tool that helps users track their cryptocurrency investments and generate tax reports.
   - **Features**: Import transactions from exchanges, track profit/loss, generate tax reports, and analyze trading performance.

- **Website**: CoinTracking

3. **Blockfolio**
    - **Overview**: A mobile app designed for tracking cryptocurrency portfolios and market news.
    - **Features**: Real-time price updates, portfolio tracking, news aggregation, and alerts for price movements.
    - **Website**: Blockfolio

4. **Delta**
    - **Overview**: A mobile app for tracking cryptocurrency portfolios and market data.
    - **Features**: Detailed portfolio tracking, real-time price updates, news aggregation, and customizable alerts.
    - **Website**: Delta

5. **CryptoCompare**
    - **Overview**: A platform that provides market data, analysis tools, and portfolio management features.
    - **Features**: Real-time data, price charts, portfolio tracking, and news updates.
    - **Website**: CryptoCompare

Conclusion

In this chapter, we have explored various tools and applications that are essential for blockchain users. From market information platforms and websites to the best cryptocurrency wallets and analysis and portfolio management tools, these resources can help you manage your assets, stay informed, and make informed decisions. By leveraging these tools, you can navigate the dynamic cryptocurrency market more effectively and enhance your investment strategies.

CHAPTER 13: NEW SOURCES AND INFORMATION

Major News Websites

Staying informed about the latest developments in the cryptocurrency and blockchain space is crucial for making informed investment decisions. Here are some major news websites that cover a broad range of financial and economic news, including cryptocurrencies:

1. **Washington Post**
   - **Overview**: A leading American daily newspaper that provides comprehensive coverage of national and international news, including finance and technology.
   - **Features**: In-depth articles, analysis, and opinion pieces on major financial developments and trends, including those related to cryptocurrencies.
   - **Website**: Washington Post

2. **Forbes**
   - **Overview**: A global media company known for its coverage of business, investing, technology, entrepreneurship, and leadership.
   - **Features**: Articles and reports on the latest trends in the cryptocurrency market,

profiles of influential figures in the industry, and insights into investment strategies.
- **Website**: Forbes

3. **Wall Street Journal**
    - **Overview**: One of the most respected financial newspapers in the world, providing in-depth coverage of the financial markets and economic news.
    - **Features**: Detailed analysis of market trends, regulatory developments, and significant events impacting the cryptocurrency and blockchain industries.
    - **Website**: Wall Street Journal

Cryptocurrency-Specific News Websites

For more focused and detailed coverage of the cryptocurrency and blockchain space, there are several dedicated news websites that provide up-to-date information, analysis, and insights:

1. **CoinDesk**
    - **Overview**: One of the most widely read news sites dedicated to Bitcoin, blockchain technology, and digital assets.
    - **Features**: Breaking news, market analysis, in-depth reports, and opinion pieces from industry experts.
    - **Website**: CoinDesk

2. **Crypto News**
    - **Overview**: A comprehensive source of news and analysis on the latest developments in the cryptocurrency market.
    - **Features**: Up-to-date news articles, market analysis, price updates, and educational content for beginners.

- **Website**: Crypto News

3. **The Block**
    - **Overview**: A research and news platform focused on providing deep insights and analysis of the cryptocurrency and blockchain industry.
    - **Features**: In-depth research reports, breaking news, market trends, and interviews with industry leaders.
    - **Website**: The Block

4. **Bitcoin Magazine**
    - **Overview**: One of the oldest and most established publications dedicated to Bitcoin and blockchain technology.
    - **Features**: Articles on Bitcoin news, technical developments, market analysis, and thought leadership from industry experts.
    - **Website**: Bitcoin Magazine

Leading Newsletters and Blogs

Subscribing to newsletters and following influential blogs can help you stay informed about the latest trends, insights, and analysis in the cryptocurrency and blockchain space:

1. **Messari**
    - **Overview**: A leading provider of crypto research and data, offering a daily newsletter with insights and analysis on the latest market trends.
    - **Features**: Market reports, research articles, and industry news.
    - **Website**: Messari

2. **The Daily Gwei**
    - **Overview**: A popular newsletter focused

on Ethereum, providing daily updates and analysis on the Ethereum ecosystem.
- **Features**: News updates, market insights, and educational content on Ethereum.
- **Website**: The Daily Gwei

3. **Decrypt**
    - **Overview**: A news website and newsletter that offers comprehensive coverage of the latest developments in the cryptocurrency and blockchain space.
    - **Features**: Daily news updates, in-depth articles, and analysis on market trends.
    - **Website**: Decrypt

4. **Coin Bureau**
    - **Overview**: A popular blog and YouTube channel that provides in-depth analysis and reviews of various cryptocurrencies and blockchain projects.
    - **Features**: Detailed articles, video content, and market insights.
    - **Website**: Coin Bureau

Social Media and Community Forums

Engaging with the cryptocurrency community through social media and forums can provide real-time updates, diverse perspectives, and valuable networking opportunities:

1. **Twitter**
    - **Overview**: A major platform for real-time news and updates from industry leaders, projects, and influencers.
    - **Features**: Follow influential figures, participate in discussions, and stay informed about the latest developments.

- **Example Accounts**: @VitalikButerin (Ethereum co-founder), @cz_binance (Binance CEO), @elonmusk (CEO of Tesla and SpaceX).

2. **Reddit**
   - **Overview**: A social news aggregation and discussion website with active communities dedicated to cryptocurrency.
   - **Features**: Subreddits like r/Bitcoin, r/Cryptocurrency, and r/Ethereum provide news, discussions, and educational resources.
   - **Website**: Reddit

3. **Telegram**
   - **Overview**: A messaging app with numerous channels and groups focused on different aspects of the cryptocurrency industry.
   - **Features**: Join groups for real-time discussions, news updates, and networking with other enthusiasts and professionals.
   - **Popular Groups**: CoinTelegraph, Crypto News, and individual project channels.

4. **Discord**
   - **Overview**: A communication platform popular with gaming and crypto communities, offering chat rooms, voice channels, and community engagement.
   - **Features**: Participate in project-specific servers, join discussions, and stay updated with announcements.
   - **Popular Servers**: CryptoPunks, DeFi Pulse, and individual project servers.

Conclusion

In this chapter, we have explored various sources of news and information that are essential for staying informed in the cryptocurrency and blockchain space. From major news websites and cryptocurrency-specific news platforms to leading newsletters, blogs, and social media communities, these resources provide valuable insights, updates, and analysis. By leveraging these tools, you can stay ahead of the curve and make well-informed decisions in the dynamic world of cryptocurrency and blockchain.

CHAPTER 14: CEX AND DEX APPLICATIONS

Centralized Exchanges (CEX)

Centralized exchanges (CEX) are platforms where cryptocurrencies are traded within a centralized infrastructure. They act as intermediaries, facilitating transactions between buyers and sellers.

1. **Binance**
   - **Overview**: Binance is one of the largest and most popular cryptocurrency exchanges in the world.
   - **Advantages**:
     - **High Liquidity**: Offers deep liquidity across a wide range of trading pairs.
     - **Wide Range of Cryptocurrencies**: Supports hundreds of cryptocurrencies and tokens.
     - **Comprehensive Trading Features**: Includes spot trading, futures, margin trading, staking, and lending.
   - **Disadvantages**:
     - **Susceptible to Stringent Regulations**: Faces regulatory scrutiny in various jurisdictions.
     - **Centralized Security Risks**: While

highly secure, centralized nature makes it a target for hackers.
- **Website**: Binance

2. **Coinbase**
    - **Overview**: Coinbase is a user-friendly cryptocurrency exchange that is particularly popular among beginners.
    - **Advantages**:
        - **User-Friendly Interface**: Intuitive design makes it easy for new users to buy and sell cryptocurrencies.
        - **High Security**: Employs strong security measures, including insurance for digital assets.
        - **Fiat Support**: Allows users to buy cryptocurrencies using fiat currencies like USD, EUR, and GBP.
    - **Disadvantages**:
        - **Relatively High Transaction Fees**: Fees can be higher compared to other exchanges.
        - **Limited Cryptocurrency Options**: Offers fewer cryptocurrencies compared to some other major exchanges.
    - **Website**: Coinbase

3. **Kraken**
    - **Overview**: Kraken is known for its strong security features and comprehensive range of trading options.
    - **Advantages**:
        - **Good Reputation**: Known for

reliability and security.
- **Advanced Security Features**: Includes measures like two-factor authentication (2FA) and cold storage.
- **Fiat Support**: Supports multiple fiat currencies for deposits and withdrawals.

○ **Disadvantages**:
- **Slow Verification Process**: Account verification can be slow, especially during high-demand periods.
- **Less Intuitive Interface for Beginners**: The platform may be less user-friendly for those new to cryptocurrency trading.

○ **Website**: Kraken

4. **Huobi**

○ **Overview**: Huobi is a major cryptocurrency exchange that offers a wide range of cryptocurrencies and trading features.

○ **Advantages**:
- **High Liquidity**: Provides deep liquidity across numerous trading pairs.
- **Wide Range of Cryptocurrencies**: Supports a large number of digital assets.
- **Staking Features**: Offers staking services for various cryptocurrencies.

○ **Disadvantages**:
- **Occasional Regulatory Issues**: Has

faced regulatory challenges in some jurisdictions.
- **High Withdrawal Fees**: Withdrawal fees can be higher than some other exchanges.
- **Website**: Huobi

Decentralized Exchanges (DEX)

Decentralized exchanges (DEX) operate without a central authority, allowing users to trade directly with each other using smart contracts on a blockchain.

1. **Uniswap**
   - **Overview**: Uniswap is a leading decentralized exchange built on the Ethereum blockchain.
   - **Advantages**:
     - **Full Decentralization**: Operates without a central authority, offering greater privacy and control.
     - **Easy to Use**: Simple interface and integration with popular Ethereum wallets like MetaMask.
     - **Integration with DeFi Wallets**: Seamlessly connects with various decentralized finance (DeFi) applications.
   - **Disadvantages**:
     - **High Ethereum Gas Fees**: Transactions can be costly due to Ethereum's high gas fees.
     - **Liquidity Can Be Low for Certain Tokens**: Smaller or newer tokens may have lower liquidity.
   - **Website**: Uniswap

2. **PancakeSwap**
   - **Overview**: PancakeSwap is a popular DEX on the Binance Smart Chain (BSC).
   - **Advantages**:
     - **Low Transaction Fees**: Lower fees compared to Ethereum-based DEXs.
     - **Wide Range of Tokens**: Supports a variety of tokens available on Binance Smart Chain.
   - **Disadvantages**:
     - **Smart Contract Risk**: As with all DeFi platforms, there is a risk associated with smart contracts.
     - **Lower Liquidity Compared to Large CEX**: While popular, liquidity may not match that of larger centralized exchanges.
   - **Website**: PancakeSwap

3. **SushiSwap**
   - **Overview**: SushiSwap is a DEX that started as a fork of Uniswap but has added additional features and innovations.
   - **Advantages**:
     - **Additional Features**: Includes lending, staking, and yield farming options.
     - **Lower Gas Fees with Arbitrum and Polygon**: Integrates with layer 2 solutions to reduce transaction costs.
   - **Disadvantages**:
     - **Smart Contract Risk**: Potential

vulnerabilities in the smart contract code.
- **Variable Liquidity**: Liquidity can vary, especially for less popular trading pairs.
- **Website**: SushiSwap

4. **Balancer**
   - **Overview**: Balancer is a DEX that allows users to create customizable liquidity pools and earn fees.
   - **Advantages**:
     - **Advanced Liquidity Pools**: Users can create pools with multiple tokens and custom weightings.
     - **Decentralization**: Operates without a central authority, enhancing security and control.
   - **Disadvantages**:
     - **Complexity of Use**: May be more complex for beginners to use effectively.
     - **High Ethereum Gas Fees**: Like other Ethereum-based DEXs, transaction costs can be high.
   - **Website**: Balancer

Conclusion

In this chapter, we have explored both centralized and decentralized exchanges, highlighting their advantages and disadvantages. Centralized exchanges like Binance, Coinbase, Kraken, and Huobi offer high liquidity, user-friendly interfaces, and a wide range of cryptocurrencies, but they come with centralized security risks and regulatory challenges. On the other hand, decentralized exchanges like Uniswap, PancakeSwap,

SushiSwap, and Balancer offer full decentralization, lower fees (especially on alternative chains like Binance Smart Chain), and integration with DeFi wallets, but they face issues like smart contract risks and variable liquidity. Understanding these platforms' features and drawbacks is crucial for selecting the right exchange based on your trading and investment needs.

CHAPTER 15: TYPES OF CRYPTOCURRENCY WALLETS

Cryptocurrency wallets are essential tools for managing digital assets, providing a way to store, send, and receive cryptocurrencies securely. There are several types of cryptocurrency wallets, each with its own advantages and disadvantages. In this chapter, we will explore the various types of wallets and their features.

Physical Wallets (Hardware Wallets)

Hardware wallets are physical devices designed to securely store private keys offline, providing a high level of security.

1. **Examples**
   - **Ledger**: One of the most popular hardware wallets, supporting a wide range of cryptocurrencies and known for its robust security features.
   - **Trezor**: Another leading hardware wallet, offering high security and a user-friendly interface.
2. **Advantages**
   - **High Security**: Private keys are stored offline, making them immune to online hacking and malware attacks.
   - **Offline Storage**: Ensures that your cryptocurrencies are safe from online

threats.
- **Support for Multiple Cryptocurrencies**: Most hardware wallets support a wide variety of digital assets.

3. **Disadvantages**
   - **Higher Initial Cost**: Hardware wallets can be expensive compared to other types of wallets.
   - **Requires Technical Understanding**: Setting up and using hardware wallets may require some technical knowledge.

Software Wallets

Software wallets are applications or programs that can be installed on a computer or mobile device, providing a convenient way to manage cryptocurrencies.

1. **Examples**
   - **Exodus**: A multi-currency wallet known for its intuitive interface and built-in exchange features.
   - **Electrum**: A lightweight Bitcoin wallet that is highly secure and fast, offering advanced features like hardware wallet integration.

2. **Advantages**
   - **Easy to Use**: User-friendly interfaces make software wallets accessible to beginners.
   - **Quick Access to Funds**: Provides quick and easy access to your cryptocurrencies.
   - **Feature-Rich**: Often includes features like built-in exchanges, portfolio tracking, and multi-currency support.

3. **Disadvantages**
   - **Vulnerable to Malware and Hacking**: Being

connected to the internet makes software wallets susceptible to online threats.
- **Requires Regular Updates**: Keeping the software updated is necessary to ensure security.

Mobile Wallets

Mobile wallets are applications designed for smartphones, allowing users to manage their cryptocurrencies on the go.

1. **Examples**
   - **Trust Wallet**: A mobile wallet that supports multiple cryptocurrencies and integrates with decentralized applications (dApps).
   - **Mycelium**: A mobile wallet known for its advanced privacy features and support for hardware wallets.
2. **Advantages**
   - **Portability**: Allows you to manage your cryptocurrencies anywhere, anytime.
   - **Ease of Use**: Mobile wallets are typically easy to use, with interfaces designed for touchscreens.
   - **Integration with dApps**: Many mobile wallets support interaction with decentralized applications.
3. **Disadvantages**
   - **Risk if Device is Lost or Stolen**: Losing your phone could result in losing access to your funds if not properly backed up.
   - **Vulnerable to Malware**: Mobile devices can be targets for malware and phishing attacks.

Web Wallets

Web wallets are online services that store your private keys and allow you to access your cryptocurrencies through a web browser.

1. **Examples**
   - **MetaMask**: A web wallet and browser extension that enables interaction with the Ethereum blockchain and its dApps.
   - **Coinbase Wallet**: An online wallet provided by Coinbase, offering a secure and user-friendly interface.

2. **Advantages**
   - **Accessibility**: Can be accessed from any device with an internet connection, making them highly convenient.
   - **Integration with dApps**: Many web wallets integrate seamlessly with decentralized applications.

3. **Disadvantages**
   - **Vulnerable to Phishing Attacks**: Web wallets can be susceptible to phishing scams where attackers trick users into revealing their private keys.
   - **Centralized Security Risks**: Trusting a third party with your private keys can introduce security vulnerabilities.

Paper Wallets

Paper wallets involve printing or writing down your private keys on a physical piece of paper, which can then be stored securely offline.

1. **Advantages**
   - **High Security if Stored Properly**: Being offline makes paper wallets immune to hacking and malware.
   - **Not Connected to the Internet**: Eliminates

the risk of online threats entirely.

2. **Disadvantages**
    - **Easy to Lose or Damage**: Physical paper can be easily lost, damaged, or destroyed.
    - **Requires Manual Setup**: Setting up a paper wallet correctly requires careful handling to ensure security.

Conclusion

In this chapter, we have explored the different types of cryptocurrency wallets, each with its own set of advantages and disadvantages. Hardware wallets offer high security with offline storage, software wallets provide convenience and ease of use, mobile wallets offer portability, web wallets provide accessibility, and paper wallets offer a high level of security if stored properly. Understanding these options allows you to choose the best wallet for your needs, balancing security, convenience, and functionality.

CHAPTER 16: MINING AND HALVING IN CRYPTOCURRENCY

What is Mining?
Definition and Purpose of Mining

Mining is the process by which new cryptocurrency coins or tokens are created and transactions are validated and added to the blockchain. It is an essential component of many blockchain networks, particularly those using Proof of Work (PoW) as their consensus mechanism.

- **Definition**: Mining involves solving complex mathematical problems to verify and record transactions on the blockchain.
- **Purpose**: The primary purposes of mining are to secure the network, validate transactions, and introduce new coins into circulation.

How it Works

1. **Transaction Verification**
   - Miners collect pending transactions from the network and organize them into blocks.
   - Each block contains a list of transactions, a timestamp, and a reference to the previous block.
2. **Solving Mathematical Problems**
   - Miners use computational power to solve

complex cryptographic puzzles.
- The first miner to solve the puzzle gets the right to add the new block to the blockchain and is rewarded with newly minted coins and transaction fees.

3. **Adding Blocks to the Blockchain**
   - Once a block is added to the blockchain, the information becomes immutable.
   - The blockchain is updated across all nodes in the network, ensuring consensus.

Types of Mining

1. **ASIC Mining**
   - **Overview**: Application-Specific Integrated Circuits (ASICs) are specialized hardware designed specifically for mining certain cryptocurrencies.
   - **Pros**: High efficiency and hash rate.
   - **Cons**: Expensive and limited to specific algorithms.

2. **GPU Mining**
   - **Overview**: Uses Graphics Processing Units (GPUs) to mine cryptocurrencies. More versatile than ASICs.
   - **Pros**: Can be used for multiple cryptocurrencies, more accessible.
   - **Cons**: Less efficient than ASICs, higher electricity consumption.

3. **CPU Mining**
   - **Overview**: Uses Central Processing Units (CPUs) for mining. Generally the least efficient method.
   - **Pros**: Accessible to anyone with a computer.

- **Cons**: Low hash rate, not profitable for most cryptocurrencies.

4. **Pool Mining**
   - **Overview**: Miners combine their computational resources to increase their chances of solving the puzzle and earning rewards.
   - **Pros**: More consistent rewards.
   - **Cons**: Rewards are divided among pool members.

5. **Solo Mining**
   - **Overview**: Mining independently without joining a pool.
   - **Pros**: Keeps the entire reward.
   - **Cons**: Highly variable and often infrequent rewards.

Impact of Mining on Prices and the Market

1. **Supply Introduction**
   - Mining introduces new coins into circulation, affecting the supply side of the market.
   - A steady increase in supply can lead to market adjustments in price.

2. **Network Security**
   - The computational power (hash rate) contributed by miners secures the network.
   - A higher hash rate generally indicates a more secure network, which can influence market confidence.

3. **Energy Consumption**
   - Mining, especially PoW, consumes

significant amounts of energy, impacting the overall cost of maintaining the blockchain.
- Environmental concerns and regulatory pressures related to energy consumption can influence market sentiment and prices.

Advantages and Disadvantages of Mining

Advantages:

- **Decentralization**: Distributes the process of transaction validation and coin creation across a wide network.
- **Security**: Contributes to the overall security and integrity of the blockchain.
- **Incentives**: Provides financial rewards for miners, incentivizing participation.

Disadvantages:

- **Energy Consumption**: High energy usage, particularly for PoW mining, leading to environmental concerns.
- **Centralization Risks**: Large mining operations can lead to centralization of mining power.
- **High Costs**: Significant initial investment in hardware and ongoing operational costs.

What is Halving?

Definition and Purpose of Halving

Halving is an event in which the reward for mining new blocks is reduced by half. This mechanism is built into the code of certain cryptocurrencies to control the supply and reduce inflation over time.

- **Definition**: Halving occurs at predetermined intervals, reducing the block reward by 50%.
- **Purpose**: To ensure a controlled release of new coins, increase scarcity, and potentially drive up the value of

the cryptocurrency.

How it Works
1. Pre-programmed Events
- Halving events are programmed into the cryptocurrency's code.
- For Bitcoin, halving occurs approximately every four years or every 210,000 blocks.

2. Reduction of Block Rewards
- When a halving event occurs, the reward that miners receive for adding a new block to the blockchain is cut in half.
- This directly reduces the rate at which new coins are introduced to the market.

Types of Halving
1. Bitcoin Halving
- Occurs every 210,000 blocks (approximately every four years).
- Historical halvings have significantly impacted Bitcoin's price and mining economics.

2. Litecoin Halving
- Occurs approximately every four years or every 840,000 blocks.
- Similar impact on price and mining as Bitcoin.

3. Bitcoin Cash Halving
- Occurs every 210,000 blocks, mirroring Bitcoin's schedule.
- Affects the supply and mining profitability of Bitcoin Cash.

4. Zcash Halving

- Occurs every four years or every 840,000 blocks.
- Reduces the block reward, impacting the supply and market dynamics.

Impact of Halving on Prices and the Market

1. Price Increase
- Historical data suggests that halving events often lead to price increases due to reduced supply and increased demand.
- Market anticipation of halving can drive speculative buying, pushing prices up before the event.

2. Mining Profitability
- Halving reduces the reward for miners, which can impact their profitability.
- Miners with high operational costs may find it unprofitable to continue, potentially reducing the network's hash rate.

3. Market Dynamics
- Reduced block rewards can lead to increased transaction fees as miners seek to maintain profitability.
- Market sentiment around halvings can lead to increased volatility.

Advantages and Disadvantages of Halving

Advantages:

- **Controlled Supply**: Reduces the rate of new coin creation, increasing scarcity and potentially driving up value.
- **Predictable Monetary Policy**: Provides a transparent and predictable schedule for changes in coin supply.
- **Incentivizes Early Adoption**: Higher initial rewards

encourage early participation and investment.

Disadvantages:
- **Reduced Miner Rewards**: Can lead to decreased mining profitability, potentially reducing network security.
- **Market Volatility**: Halving events can lead to significant price volatility, impacting market stability.
- **Increased Transaction Fees**: As block rewards decrease, miners may rely more on transaction fees, increasing costs for users.

Challenges and Opportunities in Mining and Halving

Challenges:

1. **Environmental Concerns**
   - The high energy consumption of PoW mining raises environmental concerns and regulatory scrutiny.
   - Developing more energy-efficient mining technologies and consensus mechanisms is crucial.

2. **Regulatory Pressures**
   - Governments and regulatory bodies are increasingly scrutinizing mining activities for their environmental impact and potential for illicit use.
   - Navigating regulatory environments and ensuring compliance is a significant challenge.

3. **Market Volatility**
   - Halving events can cause significant market volatility, affecting investor confidence and market stability.
   - Managing this volatility and preparing for potential market corrections is essential.

Opportunities:

1. **Innovation in Mining Technology**
   - Advances in mining hardware and alternative consensus mechanisms (e.g., Proof of Stake) offer opportunities to reduce energy consumption and improve efficiency.
   - Innovations like ASIC-resistant algorithms can promote decentralization and security.

2. **Sustainable Mining Practices**
   - Integrating renewable energy sources and sustainable practices in mining operations can address environmental concerns and reduce operational costs.
   - Initiatives like green mining can improve public perception and regulatory compliance.

3. **Market Growth and Maturity**
   - As the cryptocurrency market matures, improved infrastructure, increased institutional participation, and broader adoption present growth opportunities.
   - Halving events can catalyze market growth by increasing scarcity and driving demand.

Conclusion

Mining and halving are fundamental aspects of many cryptocurrencies, playing critical roles in their economic models and market dynamics. Understanding these processes, their impacts, and the associated challenges and opportunities is essential for anyone involved in the cryptocurrency space. By navigating the complexities of mining and halving, investors, miners, and developers can better position themselves for success in the evolving landscape of digital assets.

CHAPTER 17: THE IMPORTANCE OF NARRATIVES IN CRYPTO INVESTMENTS

Introduction to Market Narratives

In the world of cryptocurrency, market narratives play a significant role in shaping investor behavior, influencing price movements, and driving the adoption of specific technologies. Understanding and aligning with these narratives can be crucial for making informed investment decisions and maximizing returns.

What is a Market Narrative?

1. **Definition**
   - A market narrative is a story or theme that captures the collective belief of investors, developers, and users about the future potential and value of a particular technology or asset.

2. **Components**
   - **Technology**: The underlying technology and its potential applications.
   - **Use Case**: Practical applications and real-world problems the technology aims to solve.
   - **Adoption**: The level of interest and uptake

by users, developers, and institutions.
- **Regulation**: The regulatory environment and its impact on the technology's growth and adoption.

Examples of Prominent Crypto Narratives

1. **Digital Gold (Bitcoin)**
   - **Narrative**: Bitcoin is often referred to as "digital gold" due to its limited supply and store of value properties.
   - **Impact**: This narrative has driven institutional investment and adoption as a hedge against inflation and economic uncertainty.

2. **Smart Contracts (Ethereum)**
   - **Narrative**: Ethereum's smart contract functionality enables decentralized applications (dApps) and automated agreements without intermediaries.
   - **Impact**: This has positioned Ethereum as the leading platform for DeFi and NFT projects, attracting developers and investors.

3. **DeFi (Decentralized Finance)**
   - **Narrative**: DeFi aims to recreate traditional financial systems (banking, lending, trading) using decentralized blockchain technology.
   - **Impact**: The rapid growth of DeFi platforms has led to significant capital inflows and innovation in the financial sector.

4. **NFTs (Non-Fungible Tokens)**
   - **Narrative**: NFTs represent unique digital assets and ownership, revolutionizing art, gaming, and digital collectibles.

- **Impact**: This has created new revenue streams for artists and developers, while attracting mainstream attention and investment.

5. **Interoperability (Polkadot, Cosmos)**
    - **Narrative**: Interoperability solutions aim to connect different blockchains, enabling seamless transfer of assets and data across networks.
    - **Impact**: This has driven interest in projects that facilitate cross-chain interactions and scalability.

Identifying and Analyzing Narratives

1. **Research and Information Sources**
    - **News Outlets**: Follow reputable cryptocurrency news sites like CoinDesk, CryptoSlate, and The Block.
    - **Social Media**: Monitor discussions on Twitter, Reddit, and Telegram to gauge community sentiment.
    - **Industry Reports**: Read reports and analysis from research firms and industry experts.

2. **Key Indicators**
    - **Developer Activity**: High levels of development and innovation can indicate a strong narrative.
    - **Partnerships and Integrations**: Collaborations with established companies and projects can validate and strengthen a narrative.
    - **Market Trends**: Observe market trends and price movements to identify emerging narratives.

3. **Evaluating Narratives**
    - **Technology Viability**: Assess the feasibility and technical soundness of the underlying technology.
    - **Market Potential**: Consider the size and growth potential of the market addressed by the narrative.
    - **Adoption and Usage**: Evaluate the current and potential adoption by users, developers, and institutions.

Aligning Investments with Narratives

1. **Diversification**
    - Spread investments across different narratives to reduce risk and capture multiple growth opportunities.
    - Example: Invest in Bitcoin for its digital gold narrative, Ethereum for smart contracts, and Polkadot for interoperability.

2. **Long-Term Perspective**
    - Focus on narratives with strong long-term potential rather than short-term hype.
    - Example: DeFi and smart contracts have long-term applications that could transform the financial industry.

3. **Flexibility and Adaptation**
    - Stay flexible and be willing to adapt your investment strategy as new narratives emerge and existing ones evolve.
    - Example: The rise of NFTs and their impact on digital art and gaming may present new investment opportunities.

Risks and Challenges

1. **Hype and Speculation**
    - Beware of overhyped narratives driven by speculation rather than solid fundamentals.
    - Example: The 2017 ICO boom saw many projects fail due to lack of substance and viability.

2. **Regulatory Uncertainty**
    - Regulatory changes can impact the viability and growth of certain narratives.
    - Example: Increased regulation of DeFi platforms could affect their growth and adoption.

3. **Market Sentiment**
    - Narratives are often influenced by market sentiment, which can be volatile and unpredictable.
    - Example: Negative news or events can quickly shift sentiment and impact the narrative.

Conclusion

In this chapter, we have explored the importance of market narratives in the cryptocurrency space and how they influence investment decisions. By understanding and aligning with these narratives, investors can better navigate the market and capitalize on emerging opportunities. In the next chapter, we will summarize the key points discussed throughout the book and provide additional resources for further learning.

CHAPTER 18: CONCLUSION

Summary and Key Takeaways

This book has taken you on a comprehensive journey through the world of cryptocurrency and blockchain technology, from basic concepts to advanced strategies. Here are the key takeaways from each chapter:

1. **Introduction to Cryptocurrency and Blockchain**
   - **Basics**: Understanding the foundational concepts of cryptocurrencies and blockchain technology, including their significance and potential impact.
2. **Background Issues**
   - **Fiat Money**: The challenges and limitations of traditional fiat currencies, leading to the creation of cryptocurrencies as a solution.
3. **Basics of Cryptocurrency**
   - **Types of Cryptocurrencies**: Exploring Bitcoin, altcoins, and stablecoins, each with unique features and use cases.
4. **Basics of Blockchain**
   - **Technology**: How blockchain works, its key features, components, types, and real-world applications.
5. **Technology Behind Blockchain**
   - **Consensus Mechanisms**: Distributed consensus, Proof of Work vs. Proof of Stake, smart contracts, and decentralized

applications (dApps).

6. **Investing in Cryptocurrency**
    - **Investment Strategies**: Essential strategies for investing, including technical and fundamental analysis, risk management, and understanding market trends.

7. **Security in the World of Cryptocurrency**
    - **Security Practices**: Best practices for securing your cryptocurrency, types of wallets, and dealing with common security threats and scams.

8. **Regulations and Policies**
    - **Regulatory Landscape**: An overview of cryptocurrency regulations across various countries, key regulatory issues, and their impact on the market.

9. **Practical Uses of Blockchain**
    - **Applications**: Real-world applications of blockchain technology in finance, supply chain management, government, and healthcare.

10. **Future of Cryptocurrency and Blockchain**
    - **Trends**: Emerging trends, the evolution of blockchain technology, future potential, and challenges and opportunities ahead.

11. **Masterclass: Advanced Strategies for Trading and Investing**
    - **Advanced Techniques**: In-depth market analysis, new technologies, use cases, and real-world case studies.

12. **Tools and Applications for Blockchain Users**
    - **Resources**: Essential tools and applications for market information, wallets, analysis, and portfolio

management.

13. News Sources and Information
- **Staying Informed**: Major news websites, cryptocurrency-specific news platforms, leading newsletters, blogs, and social media forums.

14. CEX and DEX Applications
- **Exchanges**: Centralized and decentralized exchanges, their advantages and disadvantages, and key platforms.

15. Types of Cryptocurrency Wallets
- **Wallets**: Different types of wallets, including hardware, software, mobile, web, and paper wallets, and their security features.

16. Mining and Halving
- **Mechanisms**: The process and impact of mining and halving events on cryptocurrency supply, market dynamics, and profitability.

17. The Importance of Narratives in Crypto Investments
- **Market Narratives**: Understanding, identifying, and aligning investments with market narratives, and the risks and challenges involved.

Additional Resources for Further Learning

To continue your education and stay updated with the latest developments in cryptocurrency and blockchain, consider exploring the following resources:

1. **Books**
   - "Mastering Bitcoin" by Andreas M. Antonopoulos
   - "Blockchain Basics" by Daniel Drescher
   - "The Basics of Bitcoins and Blockchains" by Antony Lewis

2. **Online Courses**
    - "Bitcoin and Cryptocurrency Technologies" by Princeton University (Coursera)
    - "Blockchain Basics" by ConsenSys Academy
    - "Introduction to Digital Currencies" by the University of Nicosia

3. **Websites**
    - CoinMarketCap
    - CoinGecko
    - CryptoSlate
    - Token Terminal
    - Chain Broker

4. **News Outlets**
    - CoinDesk
    - Crypto News
    - The Block
    - Bitcoin Magazine

5. **Communities and Forums**
    - Reddit
    - Twitter
    - Telegram
    - Discord

6. **Newsletters and Blogs**
    - Messari
    - The Daily Gwei
    - Decrypt
    - Coin Bureau

Final Words

The world of cryptocurrency and blockchain is vast, dynamic, and full of potential. As you continue your journey, remember that continuous learning and staying informed are key to navigating this ever-evolving landscape. This book has provided you with a comprehensive foundation, but the real exploration begins as you apply these insights and engage with the community.

Embrace the opportunities, understand the risks, and remain adaptable. The future of finance and technology is being shaped by these innovations, and your participation can contribute to the transformative power of blockchain and cryptocurrency.

Thank you for embarking on this journey with "Crypto and Blockchain for Everyone: A Guide from Basics to Expert." We hope this guide has equipped you with the knowledge and confidence to navigate the world of digital finance successfully.

APPENDIX

Glossary of Cryptocurrency and Blockchain Terms

Address
- A unique string of characters used to send and receive cryptocurrency.

Altcoin
- Any cryptocurrency other than Bitcoin.

ASIC (Application-Specific Integrated Circuit)
- Specialized hardware designed specifically for mining certain cryptocurrencies.

Block
- A collection of transactions recorded on the blockchain.

Blockchain
- A decentralized digital ledger that records transactions across multiple computers.

Consensus Mechanism
- A method used by blockchain networks to agree on the validity of transactions. Examples include Proof of Work (PoW) and Proof of Stake (PoS).

Cryptocurrency
- A digital or virtual currency that uses cryptography for security.

dApp (Decentralized Application)
- An application that runs on a blockchain network, often utilizing smart contracts.

DeFi (Decentralized Finance)
- Financial services built on blockchain technology that operate without traditional intermediaries like banks.

Fiat Money
- Government-issued currency that is not backed by a physical commodity.

Halving
- An event where the reward for mining new blocks is reduced by half, controlling the supply and inflation of the cryptocurrency.

Hash Rate
- The measure of computational power used in mining.

ICO (Initial Coin Offering)
- A fundraising method where new cryptocurrencies are sold to early investors.

Mining
- The process of validating transactions and adding them to the blockchain, typically rewarded with new coins.

NFT (Non-Fungible Token)
- A unique digital asset verified using blockchain technology, representing ownership of a digital or physical item.

Private Key
- A secret key used to sign transactions and access cryptocurrency stored in a wallet.

Proof of Stake (PoS)
- A consensus mechanism where validators are chosen based on the number of coins they hold and are willing to "stake" as collateral.

Proof of Work (PoW)

- A consensus mechanism where miners solve complex mathematical problems to validate transactions and create new blocks.

Smart Contract
- A self-executing contract with the terms of the agreement directly written into code.

Stablecoin
- A cryptocurrency pegged to a stable asset like fiat currency to reduce price volatility.

Wallet
- A digital tool used to store, send, and receive cryptocurrencies. Types include hardware, software, mobile, web, and paper wallets.

References

1. **Books**
   - Antonopoulos, Andreas M. "Mastering Bitcoin: Unlocking Digital Cryptocurrencies." O'Reilly Media, 2014.
   - Drescher, Daniel. "Blockchain Basics: A Non-Technical Introduction in 25 Steps." Apress, 2017.
   - Lewis, Antony. "The Basics of Bitcoins and Blockchains: An Introduction to Cryptocurrencies and the Technology that Powers Them." Mango, 2018.

2. **Websites**
   - CoinMarketCap
   - CoinGecko
   - CryptoSlate
   - Token Terminal
   - Chain Broker

- CoinDesk
- Crypto News
- The Block
- Bitcoin Magazine

3. **Courses**
   - "Bitcoin and Cryptocurrency Technologies" by Princeton University (Coursera)
   - "Blockchain Basics" by ConsenSys Academy
   - "Introduction to Digital Currencies" by the University of Nicosia

4. **Newsletters and Blogs**
   - Messari
   - The Daily Gwei
   - Decrypt
   - Coin Bureau

Index

- **Address**: Glossary
- **Algorithmic Trading**: Chapter 11
- **Altcoin**: Glossary, Chapter 3
- **ASIC Mining**: Chapter 16
- **Bitcoin**: Chapter 2, Chapter 3, Chapter 16
- **Blockchain**: Chapter 1, Chapter 4, Chapter 5
- **Centralized Exchanges (CEX)**: Chapter 14
- **Consensus Mechanism**: Chapter 5
- **Cryptocurrency**: Glossary, Chapter 1, Chapter 3
- **dApp (Decentralized Application)**: Chapter 5, Chapter 14
- **DeFi (Decentralized Finance)**: Chapter 5, Chapter 7, Chapter 11, Chapter 17
- **Fiat Money**: Chapter 2

- **Halving**: Chapter 16
- **Hash Rate**: Chapter 16
- **ICO (Initial Coin Offering)**: Glossary, Chapter 8
- **Interoperability**: Chapter 10, Chapter 17
- **Market Narrative**: Chapter 17
- **Mining**: Chapter 16
- **NFT (Non-Fungible Token)**: Chapter 10, Chapter 17
- **Private Key**: Glossary, Chapter 7, Chapter 15
- **Proof of Stake (PoS)**: Chapter 5, Chapter 16
- **Proof of Work (PoW)**: Chapter 5, Chapter 16
- **Smart Contract**: Chapter 5, Chapter 14
- **Stablecoin**: Chapter 3
- **Technical Analysis**: Chapter 6, Chapter 11
- **Wallet**: Chapter 7, Chapter 15

Conclusion

This appendix provides a comprehensive glossary of terms, references for further reading and learning, and an index to help navigate the book's contents. By understanding the terminology and leveraging the provided resources, you can deepen your knowledge and stay informed about the latest developments in the dynamic world of cryptocurrency and blockchain.

ABOUT THE AUTHOR

Daniel Wijaya

is an interior designer, graduated from a university in Indonesia. Owner of DW Interior Design and has a spiritual YouTube channel www.youtube.com/@danielwijaya85. He wants to share his life story from childhood, when he was a teenager and when he entered the world of work, how to deal with fluctuating weight,  bullying from people around him, finding love in life, how to have a healthy diet and stable results and what written in God's word. All of these stories are obtained purely from personal experience

www.ingramcontent.com/pod-product-compliance
Lightning Source LLC
Chambersburg PA
CBHW072051230526
45479CB00010B/667